ACTING
SHAKESPEARE
& His Contemporaries

ACTING
SHAKESPEARE
& His Contemporaries

Kurt Daw

HEINEMANN • Portsmouth, NH

HEINEMANN
A division of Reed Elsevier Inc.
361 Hanover Street
Portsmouth, NH 03801–3912

Offices and agents throughout the world

Library of Congress Cataloging-in-Publication Data
Daw, Kurt.
    Acting Shakespeare and his contemporaries / Kurt Daw.
       p.   cm.
    Includes bibliographical references.
    ISBN 0-325-00054-9
    1. Shakespeare, William, 1564–1616—Dramatic production.
    2. Shakespeare, William, 1564–1616—Contemporaries.
    3. Acting. I. Title.
PR3091.D32   1998
792.9'5'09421—dc21
                                  97-52067
                                      CIP

Editor: Lisa A. Barnett
Production: Abigail M. Heim
Cover design: Julie Nelson Gould
Manufacturing: Louise Richardson

Printed in the United States of America on acid free paper

02   01   00   99   98   DA   1   2   3   4   5   6   7   8   9

Once again,
for Hillary and David

![C]ontents

Acknowledgments

I have many people to thank for their encouragement and support while writing this book. First, I must thank Lois Potter whose superb leadership of a 1992–93 National Endowment for the Arts Institute at the Folger Institute titled "Shakespeare and the Languages of Performance" was the direct inspiration for this book. For her continued friendship and encouragement, I am most grateful. I also wish to thank the members of that institute for their good company, challenging discussion and wonderful scholarship. Thanks, then, to Sally Banes, Stephen Buhler, Ann Christensen, Ann Jennalie Cook, Mary Corrigan, Eva Hooker, Geri Jacobs, David Kranz, Tom MacCary, Deborah Montuori, Kate Pogue, Milla Riggio, David Sauer, Michael Shea, Lyn Tribble, and Garry Walton. The Folger Institute staff led by Lena Cowen Orlin, and including Kathleen Lynch and Carol Brobeck, were like members of the group, and I want to thank them for their long term interest in my work and their always supportive attitudes.

Likewise I want to thank my friends and colleagues in the 1995–96 "Shakespeare Examined Through Performance" Institute, also at the Folger under the auspices of the National Endowment for the Humanities. This workshop was led by Alan Dessen and Audrey

Stanley, both of whom influenced my work and investigations deeply. The participants in this workshop, most of whom read and commented on this work in its formative stages, include Cezarija Abartis, Eric Binnie, Sheila Cavanagh, Daniel Colvin, Tom Gandy, Miranda Johnson-Haddad, Edward Isser, Robert Lane, Caroline McManus, Paul Nelsen, Ellen Summers, William Taylor and Clare-Marie Wall. I owe a special and deep measure of gratitude to Julia Matthews, who was a member of this institute and soon after became my colleague at Kennesaw State University.

I thank the rest of my friends and colleagues at Kennesaw State University, as well, especially Ming Chen and JoAllen Bradham who kindly allowed me to use photographs from their collections for this book.

Lisa Barnett has been a terrific editor, a part of a fine team at Heinemann who have been good to me throughout this process. I also want to thank the folks at Colophon, who edited and produced this book.

Finally, I want to thank the members of my family. My parents, Ken and Bula, and brothers, Chuck, Kris and Craig, are always encouraging. My father-in-law, Tom Hight, continues to show me the greatest kindness imaginable. His detailed interest and daily encouragement keep my spirits high. My wife, Hillary, and my son, David, give so much love, help and inspiration that I cannot hope words will be able to convey my gratitude. When all is said and done I know my late grandmother, Fern Prior, is the reason I do what I do. Wherever she is now, I hope she knows how much she meant to me.

Introduction

T he task of the actor is to find a way to bring to life the words and ideas of a text. To do so in a play by Shakespeare (or one of the many superb writers whose work is contemporary to his) is not so much a different kind of challenge than performing literature of our time, as it is a different magnitude of that challenge. Acting is still acting, but to do so in these plays—widely held to be the best ever written in the English language—presents actors with new (and often unfamiliar) levels of work.

This is a book written to help actors new to Shakespeare identify the special problems presented by the material and to help them structure an approach to addressing these problems. It doesn't have all the answers. It doesn't even propose that there *is* a single set of answers. There is no special set of tricks or certain stylistic approach to be applied every time a play from the period comes along.

This text is written out of a belief that there are a wide variety of creative approaches to making these beautiful plays speak to each new audience. It is born from a love for acting in plays by Shakespeare and his contemporaries and from a deeply held tenet that doing so is among the most rewarding things one can do in the theater.

What follows is not a set of all-purpose recipes, but rather a structured way to *explore* playing Shakespeare and works by his contemporaries. One of its main purposes is to alleviate what Professor Paul Nelsen wonderfully labels "ShakesFear." It outlines a plan for looking more deeply into this rewarding field. The goal is to give you a way to discover for yourself, without the hindrance of unnecessary awe, how the plays work and the growth that can come from performing in them.

How This Book Works

This book presumes that you already know something about acting, but not necessarily anything about performing Shakespeare.[1] It is written in three large parts that support each other. Rather than reading them sequentially, you may well find yourself skipping about from part to part. This is not only allowed, it is suggested. Here is how the parts interrelate:

Part I: This section of the book is here to help you understand how a play by Shakespeare *works*. It examines the structure and form of the plays and discusses how these can become the foundation of your performance. Though these may, at first, be intimidating, they are aids to your performance. The chapter then deals with preparing the text for performance. It discusses things such as how to scan the verse and how the rhetorical devices the authors use can aid you in performance. It is possible that you already know a great deal about the plays, *as literature*, and can skip over this section or consult it only lightly as needed. If, however, these are new concerns for you, then start here.

Part II: The next section begins with a warm-up and then continues with a series of acting explorations—first of a sonnet, then a monologue, then a scene, and finally a scene in a public context. This is really the heart of the book. This section is full of things *to do*, as that is how you learn to act. It explores how you embody a Shakespeare character and the way that contemporary acting concerns, such as intentions and psychological characterization, interact with the technical elements of early modern texts. In the doing, you may well discover that you need some of the information in the other sections. By all means, skip ahead and read the supporting material.

Part III: This section gives some quick but useful background information about Shakespeare's biography. It also covers the conditions of the theater of his time and how they shaped the works of authors of the period. It ends by looking at Shakespearean performance in our time. It will be especially useful after you have had an opportunity to work on the acting exercises and find yourself wanting to know more about Shakespeare and his times. Consult it whenever your curiosity dictates.

There is also a companion volume to this book, which reviews Shakespeare's plays and offers suggestions for extractable material. It also surveys some of the major authors working in Shakespeare's period and their works. It is intended to help with the perennial problem of finding good scenes and speeches for exercise work. Few of us have the kind of intimate knowledge of the whole canon needed to quickly locate just the right piece. This volume may be less useful for those who have already studied early modern drama extensively in literature courses, but it will come in handy for those who are just committing themselves to learning the canon.

As a quick example of how these sections and volumes may work together, you may want to consult the companion volume for some ideas about which sonnet to choose as you get ready to do your first acting exercise in Part II. This, in turn, may be prepared by using information gathered from Part I.

Begin, therefore, by looking quickly through the whole book. Get an idea of the general contents. As mentioned, the heart of the book is Part II, but feel free to consult other sections whenever more information is needed.

What to Call the When

A small but persistent problem for a book discussing Shakespeare and his era is what to call the time period. For a variety of reasons, *Renaissance* has fallen from favor. It is, among other things, not a particularly useful term for describing the development of England. *Elizabethan* is frequently used in senses covering all Tudor and Stuart times, but it is needed in any discussion of Shakespeare to mean the specific period of the reign of Queen Elizabeth I, which ended in the middle of Shakespeare's productive life. *Jacobean,* the counterpart term, usefully describes the later years of the time, once James had assumed the throne. It becomes cumbersome to refer to everything in the time as "Elizabethan and Jacobean," however. (*Acting in Elizabethan and Jacobean Drama* was one potential title for this book, but it certainly lacks punch.)

The most frequent solution to the problem is to call the period *Shakespearean,* but this does not help much with the discussion of his contemporary authors, which is when the term is most needed. It would lead to sentences such as, "Shakespeare and other Shakespearean-era authors used verse more extensively than is common in our time."

My solution, not always perfectly comfortable, is to adopt the somewhat scholarly term for the period and call it *the early modern period*. The advantage here is that it introduces and reinforces a term that is used throughout the critical literature that actors will eventually find themselves consulting. The disadvantage, of course, is that contrasts are frequently made between "early modern" (Shakespeare's time) and "modern" (nineteenth and twentieth century) conventions in the theater. Finding none of the other terms less problematic, I eventually adopted this one and tried to reduce the number of times I had to use these two terms in comparison to each other.

Nonsexist Acting

It is important to make one final assumption clear before you launch into Part I. Like most books now, this one makes an attempt to employ nonsexist terminology throughout. Because they are cumbersome, formulations such as "him or her" and "s/he" have been supplanted by the use of one gender or the other, in an alternating fashion, where it is feasible to do so. The term *actor* is used absolutely neutrally, implying nothing about the gender of the performer.

This book is also built around a more complex notion of nonsexist *acting*. There is no good reason, in any of the exercises in this book, for actors to limit themselves to roles with surface genders the same as their own. In fact, almost all the good reasons argue against this.

Foremost, it must be acknowledged that in Shakespeare's own time, women were forbidden to appear on stage, so all roles—whether gendered male or female—were performed by men. (The standard explanation, that adult men played the male roles and boys whose voices had not changed played the female ones, really won't stand up to scrutiny anymore. The records are unambiguously clear that men played the female roles well into their twenties.) The result of this bizarre historic circumstance is that the plays all have a certain openness to the issues of gender and a certain ambiguity about the nature of gender.

For contemporary students, it opens a lot of possibilities to treat the historic circumstance as an invitation for everybody to play everything. In training, there is no reason that women should limit themselves to "female" roles. Because there are fewer of these roles and they are smaller, this is an unfair burden. The great speeches are open to everybody. At the same time, men miss out on some of the most interesting dynamics of Shakespeare if they never experiment with the nature of those female roles in their original performance conditions.

Great care has gone into trying to avoid any implication that there are "boy" roles and "girl" roles, but unfortunately this is relatively invisible in the text. (Perhaps it would be clearer if the gender of every character were referenced in the narrative as s/he, but that is not only cumbersome, it is misleading. I am not suggesting that the *characters* don't have gender, but that, at least within training exercises, it doesn't matter who plays them.) In training, this openness is assumed to be a given.

The profession is growing more open to nontraditional casting across gender lines as well, though it is still less open than I, at least, would like to see.[2] I urge the women who train with me to be aggressive about auditioning for roles traditionally gendered male if the roles are interesting and they want to play them. Sometimes they are cast, sometimes not. I have reason to believe that they make a strong impression in any case.

Final Word About Nontraditional Casting

It should go without saying, but perhaps can't yet, that the plays of Shakespeare and his contemporaries ought to be open to actors of any race and national origin. These plays are *not* the exclusive property of actors of British descent. They are not even solely for native speakers of English. They are for everybody. Period.

Notes

1. If you have no previous acting training, you may be interested in first looking through my book on that topic: *Acting: Thought into Action*, Portsmouth, NH: Heinemann, 1997.

2. In this particular case, I do have experience to back up my opinions. In my own productions, I have usefully employed cross-gender casting. In my production of *Romeo and Juliet*, for example, Jill Perry played the Prince of Verona in a way that was unambiguously female and powerful. She was, I biasedly admit, wonderful.

ACTING
SHAKESPEARE
& His Contemporaries

1 The Riches of Language

Plays of the early modern period are language-rich. For actors, the most striking difference between the kind of work that they are used to doing in the contemporary theater and the plays of Shakespeare and his contemporaries is the complexity of language encountered in the latter. The texts at first seem much more difficult, not only because of historic and scholarly reasons, but because at a very basic level there is an orientation toward language that is richer, more adventurous and more challenging than modern plays usually attempt.

When asked why this might be so, most neophytes mutter something about how this is just the way things were back then. It comes as a surprise to many of them that people didn't all speak blank verse on an everyday basis. If you read letters and diaries of the period, however, you'll find that (except for some changed grammatical rules and a somewhat different vocabulary) people communicated in just about the same ways they still do. Most exchanges are simple and straightforward.

Nor is it true that Shakespeare wrote the way he did because it was the convention of the time. It is true that plays were more frequently written in verse, but Shakespeare himself wrote one play with almost no verse in it (*Merry Wives of Windsor*), so this was certainly not a requirement. The trouble it takes to write in verse is great enough that certainly no one would have kept up the convention if it served no purpose.

But it *does* serve a purpose. Plays that employ verse, and other verbal devices of various kinds, are easier to hear and understand than are straight prose plays. This is an advantage well worth preserving even if it means that one has to go to a lot of trouble to write it.

Easier to understand? "How can that be," my students often howl when I assert this. "We can hear for ourselves that these plays are much harder to listen to and decode than contemporary entertainments," they say. That is true, but we are comparing apples and oranges. Modern media-based entertainments, especially television shows and movies (with which we are much more familiar than live plays) are primarily visual entertainments. They are aimed at the eye.

If you want to understand the advantages of Shakespeare's writing style, compare it instead to a modern form aimed (as his plays were) at the *ear*. In this case, we have to think about popular music as it is broadcast on the radio. We know this form is not visual. We may eventually see the words, if we buy the CD and read the enclosed booklet, but we rarely encounter songs this way first. What usually happens is that we hear the song, become intrigued with it, and only later see the words.

When we do finally look at the words of songs, we almost always find that they employ all the verbal devices that we find in Shakespeare. Contemporary pop lyrics are, more often than not, written in verse. They employ large amounts of rhyme, half rhyme, metaphor, wordplay, puns, and alliteration. (Rap, of course, consists almost entirely of such devices, set against the barest minimum of melody.)

Granted, the verse form is rarely as regular as in Shakespeare, but the lyrics have strong rhythmic patterns in almost all cases. About ninety percent of songs also employ a rhyme scheme. The words are often clever turns on words and phrases. Take a second to look at your handiest printed set of song lyrics and see if this is not so.

This more complex language is often called *heightened* language. It is more compact and evocative than ordinary, everyday speech. It allows the author to say more, to say it more quickly, and to imply greater depth of meaning than unadorned prose.

Figure 1. *Heightened language is more compact and evocative than ordinary, everyday speech. It allows the author to say more, say it more quickly, and imply a greater depth of meaning than unadorned prose.* Carter Reardon as Oberon and Heidi Cline as Titania in a Classic TheaterWorks production of A Midsummer Night's Dream *directed by the author. Design by Ming Chen. Photo courtesy of Ms. Chen.*

Heightened forms—those aimed at our ears—use these devices because the verse, the rhyme, the puns, and so on, are all ways to put extra information into the line. Through poetic devices it becomes easier to say more, and then to help the listener double check what was heard. If you read the last line of prose, you have no clues as to what will come next except a vague guess that the content will follow along the same line of logic. If you read a line like:

Mary had a little lamb

or less innocently:

There once was a girl from Nantucket

you have many other kinds of clues about what will come next. Because these lines have a distinct rhythmic pattern, you can guess that the next lines will follow this pattern, and therefore be about the same length.

Within a couple of lines you will probably have figured out (often subconsciously) the rhyme scheme, and your mind might well race ahead to find words that will fit into the pattern. There are suddenly many more clues than you previously had to tell you what is coming, or to confirm what you have just heard.

Verbal devices are, therefore, ways to put extra information in the line. This information concerns both extra content, as when poems use a symbolic small example to stand for a larger issue, and matters of form.

The form makes it easier for us to grasp the information. (Line length in blank verse, for example, helps subdivide a speech into convenient ten-syllable packages. Rhyme helps again, by relating two or more of those lines to each other in a memorable way.)

Here is a very simple example. First consider this short prose passage:

> The weight of a pound shall be defined as the weight of one liquid pint of water.

This little fact was tidily summed up in a poem given to me as a study aid, which I remember clearly more than twenty years later:

A pint's a pound
the world around.

Which of those are you more apt to remember? Why?

As an experiment, compare the following short passage from a prose translation of Molière's *The Misanthrope* with the same section of the play from a poetic translation. Here is the first speech of the second act in Henri van Luan's prose translation:

ALCESTE: Will you have me speak candidly to you, Madam? Well, then, I am very angry when I think of it; and I perceive that we shall have to break with each other. Yes, I should only deceive you were I to speak otherwise. Sooner or

later a rupture is unavoidable; and if I were to promise the
contrary a thousand times, I should not be able to bear
this any longer.

Here is the same speech in Neil Bartlett's witty contemporary
translation:

ALCESTE: Look, it's better if I speak to you quite frankly.
The way you're behaving begins to upset me.
I fear that the pressure of this angry courtship
Will [eventually] rupture our relationship.
I can't lie to you and must say what's in my heart;
We are, sooner or later, bound to drift apart.
Even if I promised to forgive and make up,
I wouldn't be able to prevent our break-up.

Read each out loud to an audience or class group. Immediately
afterward, ask them to write down as much dialogue as they can recall word for word.

Through such exercises and observations you can begin to understand that the use of language by Shakespeare and his contemporaries is not old-fashioned, nor outdated, but simply heightened
language for the *ear*. Modern plays are more apt to be spectacle for
the eye and therefore do not try to be clear and memorable in the
same way. The way such language operates on the listener has not
changed and is still employed in modern ear-oriented forms like
pop music.

In our time, performance of early modern plays is apt to blend
the visual and aural qualities, so that the plays are not exclusively
verbal, but they still place far more emphasis on the qualities of the
speech than does the usual play of our time.

This chapter will take up some of the issues of language and
preparation of the text, but these should not be seen as obscure
scholarly pursuits. Instead, they are the vital means through which
we will make ourselves heard and understood to an audience. They
are as relevant today as they ever were, and they continue to be extremely useful acting tools. We'll turn our attention first to issues of
verse and scansion, and then quickly move on to rhetoric.

2 The Down and Dirty Guide to Scanning Verse

Some Hints to Help with Sounding Shakespeare's Words

For actors about to speak a few of Shakespeare's lines aloud for the first time, the most intimidating thing is rarely the depth of the characterization, or the memorization, or even the unfamiliar language. Actors encounter such complications on a regular basis. It is not these things that intimidate. It is the verse. Characterization can be debated. Memory can be improved. Odd words can be looked up, often right there on the page in the extensive footnotes. But somehow word has gotten out that there is a nonnegotiable *right* way to scan verse. Rumor has created a mythology which says that *the* way is a closely guarded secret and incredibly difficult even for those who are allowed to be initiated into its mysteries. Scansion (that dreaded word!) cannot be finessed!

Such rumors are cruelly overstated. This section of the book will help anyone facing this task for the first time to learn a few simple principles that will teach them everything they have to know to get started. The good news is that *scansion isn't all that hard.* Granted, there are some fine points that can subdue even the experts, but (for the actor) most of what needs to be done is quick and easy.

What *Not* to Scan

Let us leap in right away. The first thing to know is that much of Shakespeare's and his contemporaries' writing is *not* in verse, and there is nothing to scan. Vast portions of the plays are in prose. You can tell prose on the page because it is arranged into paragraphs rather than into lines. If you look down the left margin of your page and see that every line begins with a capital, you are seeing verse. You might be surprised, however (after hearing all your life what a wonderful poet Shakespeare is), how much of the plays are *not* written in verse form.

Prose doesn't require any special treatment. Just read what is set down for you. It is automatically right.

This, of course, is not to say that the prose portions of the plays are insignificant. They may well contain brilliant ideas and cleverly employed verbal devices. The point is, simply, that these passages do not need to be formally scanned.

What Scansion Is

When you encounter parts of the plays that *are* in verse, then it is time to think about scansion. Scansion is the practice of checking the rhythm of speech written in verse. On a very fundamental level, the purpose of writing a speech in verse in the first place is not to be "poetic," but to give it a pulse that makes it easier to speak and easier to hear. The actual sound of lines written in verse can be comprehended more easily by a listener than can the sound of lines written in prose, because in addition to the tones and pitches, rhythmic clues help convey the message. (Verse is also marginally easier to speak because there are far fewer unintentional tongue twisters of the type so common in prose.) Scansion, despite the imposing sound of the word itself, is the simple practice of checking the verse to be sure you understand its rhythm. (Perhaps scansion would be less scary if we just called it "checking the rhythm.")

What kind of rhythm do Shakespeare's lines have? They get their pulse by alternating the natural patterns of accented and unaccented words or syllables. Early modern playwrights tend to arrange these patterns in a form starting with an unaccented syllable and following it with a stressed syllable. A typical line strings together five of these unstressed–STRESSED patterns. Here is an example of a famous line that follows this pattern:

He jests at scars that never felt a wound.
1   2 3   4   5 6–7 8   9   10

By numbering the syllables of this line from 1 to 10, you'll notice that all the important words (those getting stress) are on even numbers. There is only one two-syllable word in this line, and we always say it the same way, with the accent on the first syllable. I've never heard anyone say "ne-VER," and I'll bet you haven't either. It is placed in the line so that its naturally strong syllable falls on an even number. Notice that you don't have to do anything to make the line follow this pattern. Shakespeare did all the work. If you just read it, it will have the pleasant natural pulse described above.

The technical name for lines that follow this pattern is "iambic pentameter," which is also called "blank verse" if the lines don't rhyme. You'll hear these terms thrown around so much that it is useful to have heard them, but knowing them is not essential to what you have to do.

Most actors in my experience have heard this much, and even know to beat the lines out, saying something like:

de-DUM de-DUM de-DUM de-DUM de-DUM!

In doing so, they often find lines right away that fit this pattern, like:

The quality of mercy is not strained

And live we how we can, yet die we must.

In both of these cases, "scanning" the lines is just a matter of reading them, noticing the rhythm is exactly what is expected, and giving yourself a little pat on the back for knowing that. You don't *make* the lines fit the pattern; Shakespeare did that. You just read them. (The second one of these has a natural pause in the middle, which we'll want to talk about more later.)

Variations

Finding these lines and recognizing them is rewarding and confirming. The first real scansion problem arises from the fact that actors immediately find even more lines that *don't* fit this pattern. That is because Shakespeare and his contemporaries regularly employed two variations on this pattern to keep it from becoming so rhythmic as to be sing-songy.

At the beginning of a line, it is not uncommon to find the first two syllables reversed so that the line has a surprising and vigorous beginning. The pattern then becomes DUM-de de-Dum de-Dum de-Dum de-Dum. Here is a line that employs this variation:

> Now is the winter of our discontent
> 1 2 3   4-5 6   7 8– 9–10

This line, the opening of *Richard III*, starts with more energy than is usual in the pattern we had previously discussed, but the variation is slight enough to preserve the general feel of the rhythm while giving it a subtle new interest.

Here are a couple more examples:

> Doom'd for a certain term to walk the night

> Throw your mistemper'd weapons to the ground

In both of these you can hear the strength of the opening. This variation goes by the technical name of "trochaic variation," or "trochaic inversion" but even experienced actors tend to shy away from using these names. It is simply thought of as the variation that happens at the beginning of lines. Notice that you still don't have to do anything about lines employing this variation. You are not going to say "doom'd-FOR." If you read the line as you naturally would, you find that you have "scanned" it correctly, employing the natural variation.

The second variant form, like the first, requires no special action on the actor's part. It is a variation placed at the end of lines to break the monotony of marching up to a climactic final syllable every time. An extra unstressed syllable is placed at the line end (lengthening it out to eleven syllables), creating a softened impact.

The technical term for this is *feminine ending,* but the sheer political incorrectness of that is making it quickly fade from use. It is perhaps best to think of this simply as the variation that happens at the end of lines. Here are a couple of examples of lines employing this variation, using an (E) to mark the final softened syllable:

> I come to bury Caesar, not to praise him
> 1 2   3 4–5   6–7 8 9 10   (E)

> Her dotage now I do begin to pity.

Lines that employ this variation are very helpful in beating the problem created by every line banging to a halt in exactly the same manner. Rhythm is helpful in creating understanding, but it can become too predictable without subtle variation interspersed throughout.

Combinations and Caesuras

So is that all there is to it? Almost. You should know that these two variations can be used in combination. Some lines start with the first variation and conclude with the second, like:

> Free from the bondage you are in, Messala.
> 1   2   3 4–5   6 7 8   9–10–(E)

One final point needs our consideration. Remember the line with the pause in the middle?

> And live we how we can, yet die we must.

Pauses of this nature are very common in Shakespearean lines. Like everything else, it has a technical name, *caesura,* which is a word that turns out to mean "pause." These pauses are important, because both variations can happen around such a pause. That is to say, the extra syllable of the second variation can happen just before such a pause:

> And by opposing end them. To die, to sleep
> 1   2   3 – 4 – 5 6 (E) 7 8   9 10

The first variation can sometimes happen just after the pause. Here is a famous line that employs a combination of a strong beginning just after the caesura and an extra syllable at line's end. (Note beats 7 and 8 are inverted.)

> To be or not to be. That is the question.
> 1 2 3 4 5 6   7 8 9 10–(E)

Lines sometimes include variations at both the pause and at the line end:

> My father's brother, but no more like my father
> 1 2 3 4 (E) 5 6   7 8 9 10 (E)

This line actually has twelve syllables, but still meets the qualifications as normal blank verse working within the variations.

There are two important points to remember: First, these variations are employed only in two places—at the line end/beginning and at the phrase end/beginning on either side of the caesura. They never occur elsewhere in the line. (For this reason, there are never more than two examples of each kind of variation in a line.)

Second, they are temporary variations that affect only one small part of the line. In the beginning variation, there is a strong syllable followed by a weak one (backward from the normal pattern), but the rest of the line immediately returns to the normal pattern. In the line ending variation, there is an extra syllable at the end of the phrase or line, but at the next syllable, the line pattern resumes it normal shape.

In all of these cases, there is nothing for the actor to do but read the line. Normal pronunciation of the words will yield the pattern the playwright wanted. The verse can be incredibly varied, yet still retain an underlying sense of the pulse so beneficial to the listening audience.

So what is the big deal about scansion? Why does everyone act like it is so hard? You can see from the previous discussion that it isn't really difficult, though it might take a bit of practice to learn to recognize lines that employ variations to the regular pattern. To help you, let's create a checklist of what we know so far:

1. Is the line ten beats long, alternating stress and unstress? (That's the normal expectation.)

2. If not, is there a surprisingly strong start, or start to the phrase just after the pause, or both? (Then, it's normal, employing the line start variation.)
3. Is there an extra syllable at the end of the line, at the end of the phrase before the pause, or both? (Then it's normal, employing the end-of-line variation.)

All of these require recognition but no special action. There are some times that the actor must take some action, however, and we'll turn to those now.

Choice Moments

Throughout Shakespeare there are lines that require some special attention on the part of the actor. There are two usual causes for this need. One is that we often write things down in a way that is slightly more formal than the way we speak. The other is that occasionally things have changed since Shakespeare's time.

In the first case, it is very important to notice that some words look like they have more syllables than they usually do when we speak them. *Interest,* for example, looks like a three syllable word: *in-ter-est.* But in daily use, almost everyone pronounces it as a two syllable word: *in-trest.* Shakespeare writes formally but assumes you'll pronounce things the way people normally speak. His usual habit is to treat the word in its shortest form. For this reason, speakers feigning a high British accent to "class up" Shakespeare often get it especially wrong. When counting syllables, you'll notice that many words need to be treated a bit disrespectfully. (Just for the record, the technical name for this process is "elision.") Here are a couple of examples:

He hath more worthy interest to the state
1 2   3   4–5   6–7   8 9 10

Try saying this line treating *interest* as a three-syllable word, and you'll instantly see the difficulty in speaking it. It is so much smoother when *interest* is elided as in normal, everyday speech.

An honest tale speeds best being plainly told.

Did you find the necessary change? If *being* is treated as a one-syllable word (*bing*), it fits perfectly, and such is the way that people usually speak it when they are not trying too hard.

If elisions are formally noted in the text, we call them contractions. *I'd, he'd,* and *you'll* frequently appear in the text in their contracted forms, but sometimes it is left to you to elide the words, as in:

> I had rather be a dog and bay the moon

In this line, the first two words are intended to contract into "I'd." The rhythm makes that plain. Contractions often occur between two words, and not just words you're used to seeing printed in short form. *The* usually contracts into the next word if it starts with a vowel, for example: *th'interest* or *th'inconstant*. Don't be too respectful, or you can ruin the pulse. (One word of caution about contractions: a fair number of times, the contractions that *are* marked in the text are wrong. The word or words need to be spoken fully to create the rhythm. There are elaborate theories why this may be so, having to do with printers introducing changes in the text to conserve space or scribes saving time. Don't worry about why, just count the beats. If you are one beat short, it is probably because the contraction is marked incorrectly.)

So let's start a new checklist. Imagine you have encountered a line that isn't iambic pentameter, and that doesn't seem to conform to either of the two usual variations. Step one, then, is to:

1. Look for contractions or elisions.

If the line is too long, and the extra syllable occurs in midline rather than at the pause (caesura), there is probably an elision needed. Here are a couple of practice lines. See if you can find the needed corrections:

> His noble kinsman—most degenerate king!

> She is a virtuous and a reverend lady.

The following are the patterns of these lines in syllable counts. In the first line, you can see that "degenerate" needs to contract to "degen'rate." In the second line, you may have been temporarily alarmed to find thirteen syllables at first count. If you contract to "virt'chwus" and "rev'rend," you come down by two. The line then reads like a normal line, but also using both the beginning and the line end variations! Thus:

> His noble kinsman—most degenerate king!
> 1   2–3   4–5   6   7–8–9   10

> She is a virtuous and a reverend lady.
> 1   2 3   4–5   6   7 8–9   10-(E)

If the line is too short, make a quick check to see if there is an incorrect contraction marked.

Words with "v" in the Middle

There is a kind of contraction, commonly practiced in Shakespeare's time, that has now gone completely out of use. This form causes so much trouble that it needs a special category on our checklist all for itself. This is the elision of "v"s from the middle of words. We are vaguely used to seeing this in poetry in the word *ever,* which is frequently shortened to *e'er.* It shows up all the time in hymns and Christmas carols. Elision of "v"s was very common to Shakespeare's period, in many words. *Devil, evil, seven,* and *given* are all words frequently shortened in verse. Here is an example:

> From Athens is her house remote seven leagues.
> 1   2–3   4   5   6   7–8   9   10

As you can see, the line scans with *seven* as a one-syllable word—*se'en*—pronounced something like "sen." In cases like this, in consultation with your director and dramaturg, you must make a choice. The point of verse is easy intelligibility. In this case, however, honoring the rhythm may lead you to using a word that is completely incomprehensible to the listener. Most modern directors will instruct you to fully pronounce the word, but they'll appreciate your cheating it down as much as possible, to something like *sev'n.* They'll also be impressed that you know about the "v" problem. So now our checklist looks like this:

1. Look for contractions or elisions.
2. Double check for "v" words.

Expanded Word Endings

Having followed the checklist, you may still find some lines that don't seem to scan. These lines are often too short. This is because there are classes of word endings that were pronounced in expanded forms in Shakespeare's time that are sometimes shortened in our time. These are words ending in *tion* and *ed*. Words such as *diseased* and *charmed* are sometimes pronounced "dis-ease-éd" and "charm-éd" in verse lines, because they were occasionally pronounced that way in everyday use in Shakespeare's time. Here are a couple of examples:

> Death's pale flag is not advancéd there
>
> I bear a charméd life, which must not yield

Likewise, *tion* words are sometimes expanded, as in this line, in which it requires the pronunciation "im-ag-in-a-she-un":

> Such tricks hath strong imagination.

and

> The brightest heavens of invention

Here are a couple of lines from Mark Antony's eulogy for Caesar:

But Brutus says he was am/bi/ti/ous
1   2–3   4   5   6   7–8–9–10

> and Brutus is an hon/or/ab/le man.
> 1   2–3   4 5 6–7–8–9   10

These lines will again require a consultation with the director, but the usual practice is to scan them fully, because, though their sound may be odd, their meaning is still perfectly comprehensible. So now our checklist looks like this:

1. Look for contractions or elisions.
2. Double check for "v" words.
3. Look for word endings needing expansion.

Names

A final category of check points is names. Names are notoriously variable in Shakespeare, changing in pronunciation from one context to another. For example, we usually think of Shakespeare's unfortunate lovers as Rome E. Oh and Jule E. Et, but at many points in the play you'll find that their names must be pronounced more like Rome Yoh and Jule Yet. The most famous line in the play, for example, is the most often incorrectly scanned:

Romeo, Romeo, Wherefore art thou Romeo
1–2   3 –4   5– 6   7 8   9 –10

This line ends at thirteen syllables in terrible rhythm unless Romeo's name is pronounced as two syllables. (It's a bit odd even then.)

Time and time again, names in Shakespeare have a variable quality. Hermia (Herm-ya), Helena (Helen), Mercutio (Mer-cue-show), and Titania (Ti-tan-ya) are just a few examples.

Our checklist now reads:

1. Look for contractions or elisions.
2. Double check for "v" words.
3. Look for *ed* and *tion* words needing expansion.
4. Consider all names carefully. They can vary from line to line!

All of this is simple, requiring no more than a bit of practice and patience. Over ninety-nine percent of Shakespeare's lines (and those of most of his contemporaries, by the way) fit into these patterns—that is, within the bounds of the normal variations—and using the subtle adjustments listed, they can be determined to "scan" normally.

On very rare occasions you will find a word that scans in an unusual pattern because it was pronounced differently in Shakespeare's time. We usually say "ré-ven-ue," for example, but in many cases, Shakespeare said "re-vén-ue," with the stress on the second syllable.

My manors, rents, revenues I forgo;

Such deviations from contemporary practice are so rare that they are usually footnoted in modern editions of plays. In any given play, there are only three or four of these cases to be found. I was recently working on Brutus, and discovered that the following line of mine required an Elizabethan pronunciation:

Nor construe any further my neglect.

The second word has a first-syllable stress, unlike its modern form. This is actually the first line requiring such accommodation I have spoken on stage during a career nearing twenty years! It is quaint occasions like this that are trotted out to terrify young actors, but they are disproportionately rare in reality.

The "rules," then, are rather short. There are just a couple of other things you ought to know to speed you on your way. The first is that you don't always have the complete line to yourself. Many lines of verse are split between two or more speakers. When you find these, they are usually arranged on the page in a way that indicates this to you. For example:

ORLANDO: I will not touch a bit.
DUKE: Go find him out.

The indentation of the Duke's line is an indication that he is completing a verse line begun by Orlando. You must scan the whole line to understand your part.

The second is that prose lines are sometimes thrown in, right in the middle of verse passages. This is usually apparent because they are no longer arranged as verse on the page, but a line shorter than a usual verse line will leave no indication. It begins with a capital and doesn't stretch to the margin. A totally arrhythmic line is a powerful acting note, but it can be disconcerting to the beginner.

Of course, there are always exceptions to all the foregoing. Magical beings usually speak lines that are only eight syllables long in Shakespeare, and normal characters occasionally speak lines of twelve. There are a few lines that even the most dedicated scholars can't quite figure out. If you have gone through the checklist and looked at all the possibilities and you still cannot make sense of the line's form, then treat it as an acting note. A deliberately strange line is sometimes introduced to create a strange effect. The purpose of scanning is not to regularize the verse, but to understand it. If you encounter an oddity, relish it!

Very Brief Words About Speaking Verse

Scanning verse and speaking verse are very different subjects, the latter being much larger. Much of the rest of this book will concern itself with performance of verse, but before you undertake these exercises, it is appropriate to offer a few quick pointers to get you started.

1.   The first thing to know is that most beginning speakers of verse break it up into too many short units of meaning, and in doing so, they distort the form so much that all the advantages of verse disappear.

> To be,
> or not
> to be.
> That
> is the question.

Such a reading is not uncommon, but in good verse speaking, it is useful to keep the rhythm and flow going so that the listener can "hear" the form. Read to the end of the line. If the unit of meaning stops there, then take a breath at that point. If the phrase continues into the next line, then lift (or stress) the final word in the line, but continue without pausing. This practice eliminates much unnecessary waiting. I've seen a play rehearsal cut fifteen minutes out of its previous running time, just by eliminating unnecessary pauses.

2.   Verse can, and should, be spoken faster than prose. I've seen performances of Shakespeare spoken at 1200 lines per hour, as opposed to the equivalent of normal speech, which is about 700 lines per hour. I find this a tad fast for my taste, but 1000 per hour is a perfectly comfortable speed. Audiences, in fact, are rarely aware of the speed. The verse seems exciting, not rushed!

When practicing verse, work at speeds that are comfortable. By your final rehearsal, however, push yourself to speak just a tad faster than is comfortable. Your listeners will be ahead of you if you choose to talk at the same speed you do in everyday conversation.

3. Keep the energy going to the end of the line. Verse lines are almost always climactic, meaning their point sits in the last word or two. In everyday speech, however, we usually put all the important stuff at the beginning and let our sentences trail off.

When you are working with verse, it is important to reverse your usual habits. A line should grow in intensity:

In sooth, I know not why I am so sad.

This creates a sense of connection and involvement in the listener. The opposite habit, where lines trail off in the end, dismisses the listener's attention. I have often attended shows that were criticized for a slow pace, but they were, in actuality, traveling fast enough. The "end-drop" syndrome, however, made them seem interminable.

These three simple starting points are just the tip of the iceberg, but by following them, you will find that the structure of the verse (which you have worked so carefully to scan) will be clear to the listener.

3 A World of Words

When we think of the text of an early modern play, initially it is the verse that captures our attention. Arranging words into the rhythmic patterns of verse is, however, only one of the ways that writers make their words more memorable for actors, so that actors can make them more memorable for audiences.

The vast range of devices available is known collectively as *rhetoric*. Learning to use these devices is a fascinating and delightful field of study. In Shakespeare's time, rhetoric formed the basis of much of a schoolboy's education, and it remained an important part of the curriculum until the twentieth century. In our time, unfortunately, the focus has shifted from the study of successfully using these many devices. Instead, on the rare occasions rhetoric is examined at all, the goal is more about finding and categorizing devices in printed texts.

This is a chapter about rhetorical devices, but it will strive to avoid the error of too much terminology and too little joy. Instead, the emphasis here will be on the way that early modern texts help make the words memorable. There will be some labeling, but you are reminded it is using, rather than naming, devices that counts.

The following sections explore the most common, and helpful, devices in the arsenal of Shakespeare and his fellows. It is nowhere near comprehensive, but it is all you need to get you started.

Playing with Sound: Alliteration, Assonance, and Onomatopoeia

From the medieval tradition, one of the most common devices in Shakespeare is the binding together of groups of words by playing with their sounds. Finding a group of words that start with a common sound is still a frequent advertising ploy and is common in pop lyrics. Think of "Bewitched, bothered, and bewildered." The three "B" sounds tie these words together in a way that "Enchanted, obsessed, and confused" just doesn't, even if the meaning is the same. When this pattern is created by repeating consonant sounds, we call it *alliteration*. Meaning "lining up letters," this device brings an interest to lines that may otherwise get lost. Look at the following quatrain from the opening speech of *Richard III*:

> Now are our **b**rows **b**ound with victorious wreaths,
> Our **b**ruiséd arms hung up for **m**onuments,
> Our stern alarums changed to **m**erry **m**eetings
> Our dreadful **m**arches to delightful **m**easures.

Notice the way the three "B" sounds lead us from the first line to the second, and then the new emphasis on "M" sounds creates a path through the second half of the second line that lasts until the end of the quatrain.

This device is very powerful. It draws attention to words and binds them together. Shakespeare, who was not above a few jokes at his own expense, was aware of this. He parodies his own technique, taken to an extreme so that it becomes a joke, in the naive play-within-a-play scene from *A Midsummer Night's Dream*:

> What dreadful dole is here?
> Eyes, do you see?
> How can it be?
> O dainty duck, oh dear!
> Thy mantle good,
> What, stained with blood?

> Approach, ye furies fell.
> O fates, come, come
> Cut thread and thrum,
> Quail, crush, conclude and quell.

A subtler form of the same idea is when words are aligned by selecting similar vowel sounds within them. This is called *assonance* and is generally much less noticeable in performance. An example of a line driven by such concerns, however, might be the opening of Macbeth's dagger soliloquy:

> Is this a dagger I **see** before me,
> The **handle** toward my **hand**?

In this line, there is a very noticeable dependence on vowels, which, as couriers of emotion, help launch Macbeth into his hallucinatory frenzy.

Onomatopoeia is the device whereby the word sounds like the thing or action it is describing. *Zip*, *ping*, and *pop* are words with this quality. In performance, it is exciting when this device is brought into play, as in Lear's great storm speech:

> **Blow,** winds, and **crack** your cheeks! **Rage, blow**
> Your cataracts and hurricanoes, **spout**
> Till you have **drenched** our steeples, **drowned** our cocks!

The point of all three devices is to manipulate sound into helping create a greater sense of meaning and unity, not to find and name examples. When you find them, however, you will recognize quickly the power they hold in performance.

Comparing and Contrasting: Antithesis

In his book, *Playing Shakespeare*, The Royal Shakespeare Company's John Barton says that if he could teach only one device to a young actor, this would be it. Antithesis is the setting up of opposites. This is done by pairing examples, such as this example from *Macbeth*:

> So **foul** and **fair** a day I have not seen.

Technically, the first half of the pair is called the thesis, and when its opposite is brought into play, that is the *anti*-thesis, but most actors refer to one pair as an example of antithesis. The plural of this is antitheses.

It is absolutely stunning, once you become aware of the device, how often it is used in Shakespeare and plays of his time. *Most* long speeches are built on it. Frequently there are many pairs of antitheses deployed in a speech.

To use this device, it is important to emphasize the two parts, bringing equal stress to each. It helps, when beginning, to treat the two halves as items being balanced in a scale and to use literal gestures to set them forth.

It is hard to find an extended passage in Shakespeare that does not contain an example of this device, but for the multitude, let this one example stand. It also is from *Macbeth*:

> That which has made them **drunk,** has made me **bold**
> What hath **quench'd** them, hath given me **fire**.

In this two-line passage, Lady Macbeth contrasts the courage she has taken from the wine to the inebriation it has caused the unnamed drinkers. She repeats such telling imagery in the second line when she contrasts the usual property of liquids (its ability to quench) to the very surprising outcome it has had in her (it has set her, metaphorically, afire). The speed with which her condition is so memorably described is astonishing.

If you do nothing else, practice this device. It will clarify more in Shakespearean (and other early modern) texts than anything else you can do.

Double Entendre: Bawdy

They say there is no accounting for taste. It sometimes seems that taste for the indelicate pun and the dirty joke is more unaccountable than all other forms of taste combined. Our popular media is filled with sexual innuendo on various levels of subtlety, and has been for decades, with public acceptance or condemnation frequently alternating. Sometimes we find this amusing, but sometimes we are shocked by it.

Shakespeare lived in an era in which sexual frankness was coming up against strong (literal) puritan objection. There can be little doubt where he stood, as his plays are filled with *bawdy* or mildly off-color jokes and puns. Many of these we no longer get, because the double meaning is lost to us. Shakespeare's own name, Will, for example, was also used in his time to mean sexual desire. He more than once puns on his own name in the plays.

Because these jokes can take a great deal of explaining, they seem at first not to be worth pursuing, but because (when offered in the right spirit and monitored with just enough taste) they bring life and humor to the plays, they can greatly alter one's approach.

The definitive guide to the matter of double meaning is Partridge's *Shakespeare's Bawdy*, which lists 200 pages worth of definitions. It is an indispensable actors tool, in part because most other editions are very reluctant to footnote even the most blatant examples. Many an obscure passage is indecipherable until you discover it is built on sexual punning that is not explained.

The point of such passages is not just to be titillating. *Romeo and Juliet* is shot through with such punning, in part to help us see that the star-crossed lovers feel more for each other than the lust their friends feel. Both Mercutio and the Nurse talk incessantly, and ribaldly, of sex. Their chief function is to serve as contrasts to Romeo and Juliet's loftier conceptions of human relationships.

The real trick to bawdy is to see that it remains *double* entendre. Punning passages have a perfectly comprehensible surface meaning which must not get lost. It may take some time and experience to discover how far to go toward the joke and how much to play the surface meaning. Like many performance problems, it is a question of balance.

Creating Excitement: Builds

There are literally dozens of technical names for various kinds of *builds* in rhetoric, depending on the nature and style of the build, but the basic theory behind them all is that ideas are not just strung around a speech in random order, but are arranged in some escalating order of magnitude or meaning. It is a kind of rhetorical ladder to be climbed incrementally.

Here is an example. It is Ariel, a magical spirit, describing the way in which he turned himself into illusions on board a ship full of men he was attempting to frighten:

> I boarded the King's ship. Now on the beak,
> now in the waste, the deck, in every cabin,

I flamed amazement. Sometime I'd divide,
And burn in many places; on the top-mast,
The yards, and the bowsprit, would I flame distinctly;
Then meet and join. Jove's lightening, the precursors
O'th' dreadful thunderclaps, more momentary
and sight-outrunning were not. The fire and cracks
Of sulfurous roaring the most mighty Neptune
Seems to besiege, and make his bold waves tremble,
Yea, his dread trident shake.

In this speech, we see the structure of two builds. The first one is a list of places Ariel flamed. It is a climactic list: first the prow, then (even better) the mid-ship, then (better yet) the deck, and finally (best of all) in the cabins. There is no point in making a list like this unless each step is better than the last. In this case, we can see that Ariel started his antics at the very tip of the ship, and as the men grew more afraid and fled deeper into the ship, he invaded more space, including their very cabins, where we imagine they have fled hoping closed doors would protect them. As Ariel tells this, it is important that he convey his mounting glee at doing the work better and better. He "climbs this ladder" in a careful, step-by-step fashion, with every increment spelled out.

He then goes into a second build—a list of appearances he made. It starts with dividing into several small flames, then (even better) reassembling into a big flame, then (better yet) turning into lightning, and finally (best yet) into a full-blown storm that was like Neptune in full anger.

Beginning actors are apt to make the mistake of just listing items. What is important in such a list, however, is that it keeps getting better. It is like telling a great story, when you delay the punch line until the last moment. Everything builds up to the point. Climb the ladder one step at a time to arrive at the top.

There are a number of ways to accomplish a build technically. Sir Laurence Olivier was famous for builds wherein, on each item in the list, he raised his voice one pitch on a chromatic scale. Volume and energy can be used, just as pitch, in increasing amounts.

My experience tells me that the main way to achieve this effect, however, is just to analyze how the list is accomplished. How do the items relate to each other? As soon as you see how they grow in importance, your voice will reflect your desire to communicate this.

Images: Metaphor and Simile

One of the ways that verse and poetry become most memorable is by casting their ideas into forms that evoke specific *images* in the minds of the listeners. When Romeo says Juliet is the sun, he is telling us how completely she represents life to him. Because he says she *is* that thing, rather than *like* it, he is employing a *simile*. Juliet returns the intensity of that image when she later says that Romeo is the god of her idolatry.

If the comparison is made more explicit, by employing the use of the words *like* or *as,* then the form is a *metaphor.* An example might be the first line of Sonnet 23, "As an unperfect actor on the stage," where the poet is specifically comparing himself to a forgetful actor. That is a memorable image when the point is that he is simply a tongue-tied lover. He is so taken with his friend's beauty that he is temporarily struck dumb. It is *like* the stage fright of an actor.

Images need to be realized on the stage. They require that the actor take the time to imagine fully what is being described, and call from his or her own experience a suitable example to draw on in performance.

Images make memorable the mundane. Juliet is, in modern terms, "awesome." She looks great, and Romeo is very taken with her. We don't understand how completely, however, until he employs his sun image. Then we see what a big deal this is!

Rhyme, Half-rhyme and Historic Rhyme

The last device at which we shall look, perhaps the most powerful of all, is *rhyme.* We were first introduced to this concept when we were just children, when it served the important function of helping us conceptualize sound and sense similarities.

Rhyme is, of course, when words sound alike. It is used in Shakespeare plays often, though in some much more than in others. Rhyme is generally employed at the end of lines, though sometimes lines have rhyming words within them, which give them an impression of extra speed in delivery.

In long passages of rhyme, such as one encounters in *Love's Labour's Lost,* the effect is of sparkling brilliance of thought. More commonly, we get couplets planted near the end of scenes to summarize the main plot point or, especially, to point us toward the upcoming scene. Here is one from *Comedy of Errors:*

> Since mine own doors refuse to entertain me,
> I'll knock elsewhere, to see if they'll disdain me.

For reasons beyond his comprehension, a man has been refused entry to his own home, and he sums up his predicament with this little couplet before setting off to see if he can discover what is wrong. These tidy summaries occur near the end of most Shakespeare scenes and are major guideposts for actors and audience alike. They help us to be sure what the point of this scene is and let us anticipate the next one. It is the rhyme that makes them stand out from the lines all around them, rendering them memorable.

Sometimes the playwright wants to soften this effect slightly and uses what we call half-rhyme—words that almost rhyme. Their effect is to tickle the ear without assaulting it. *Room* and *soon* are such a pair. They don't really rhyme, but if placed at line ends, they tease us.

Much more common in Shakespeare are lines that, because of changing pronunciation, once rhymed but no longer do. One of Shakespeare's favorite rhymes is *love* with *prove*, words that were both pronounced just enough differently in his time as to rhyme with each other. These are called historic rhymes. There are many of these in the plays. Words like *history* and *victory*, for example, used to end with a long "I" sound, rhyming with *die.* (The old pronunciation is preserved in our word *try.*)

We usually don't try to capture historic rhymes on the stage anymore, except when we want a humorous effect. (In the *Midsummer Night's Dream* example at the beginning of the chapter, there is an historic rhyme—"Thy mantle good/What, stained with blood?"—where, for the joke, *blood* is often changed to rhyme with *good.* It so happens, of course, that originally this was no joke. The lines really rhymed!)

The fact that we are not going to try to spell out the rhymes for the audience doesn't change the fact that they can be very helpful to us in spotting lines that Shakespeare particularly wanted to make memorable. We owe them extra attention, even if we will not be pronouncing them in a way that reinforces the ear.

Summary

There are literally hundreds more devices that are sometimes employed, but if you attend to the ones provided in this chapter, and relish them, you will find both your pleasure in performing them and the audience's comprehension rising.

Keep these devices in mind as you approach the next few chapters, which contain the acting exercises. These are built on the backs of the physical, vocal, and textual preparations you have accomplished so far.

Further Reading

If you want to know more about this subject, I recommend:

Brubaker, E.S. 1976. *Shakespeare Aloud: A Guide to His Verse on Stage.* Lancaster, PA: Published by the Author.

This little book (from which many of the examples in this chapter are taken) covers the whole subject in greater depth but is still clear enough to be accessible to beginners. For those interested in the advanced lesson, look at:

Spain, Delbert. 1988. *Shakespeare Sounded Soundly: The Verse Structure & the Language.* Santa Barbara, CA: Garland-Clarke Editions/Capra Press.

---

exercises

---

1. Look up parallel passages from a prose and a verse translation of a play. (Molière is widely available, but Spanish drama also works well for this.) Read the passages aloud to compare their comprehensibility and memorability.
2. Find examples from your own contemporary music collection of song lyrics that use the devices described in this chapter. Trade examples with others. Get used to noticing that verse devices are common in our time, not just in Shakespeare's.

4   A Quick Voice and Body Warm-up

Acting is first and foremost a physical discipline. It requires intense effort, often much more than the neophyte imagines. The plays of Shakespeare and his contemporaries are particularly active, far more than the average play of our time. The plots of these plays from the early modern period often call for such physically demanding activities as dancing, swordplay, unarmed combat, and chase scenes. They are also longer, in general, than plays of more recent composition.

They require a great deal of vocal energy as well. The plays are rhetorically-based; words cascade forth where modern plays use fewer, simpler words or even silence. To perform them well requires the intense commitment of energy from the lips, tongue, vocal apparatus, and breath mechanism.

The purpose of this chapter is to help you learn to warm-up your voice and body, to experience the nature and level of physical and vocal involvement, and to explore your acting instrument in the context of Shakespearean drama and other plays of his period.

The exercises that follow are, of course, just a starting point. Whole books have been written on these subjects. (Some of the best of these are recommended in the Further Reading section at the end of the chapter.) Neither this nor any chapter can replace study with a trained, expert teacher. The exercises constitute neither a voice nor a movement class, but form a series you can use in slow, deliberate fashion to begin developing your instrument or truncate into a warm-up. (If you want to pursue acting professionally, of course, work with an experienced teacher is probably necessary at some point in your study.) What follows is intended as an introduction for the beginner, or a refresher for the more experienced. For all, it is to be hoped that these exercises will be relaxing and enjoyable.

What Voice?

Before beginning any vocal exercises, it is important to clarify a basic premise of the work that follows. The voice to use in performance is *your* voice, not an imitation of the "Shakespearean" voices you may have heard on recordings or in films. Ironically, the stereotypical "Received Pronunciation" accent adopted by many beginning students has no historic authority whatsoever.

We can recreate the sound of the language as Shakespeare and his fellow actors would have spoken it, but it is rather unlike any of the major dialects spoken anywhere in the world today. It is best preserved in the isolated Appalachian communities of the southern United States, which were founded by immigrants from England at about the time Shakespeare was writing. It is a rough, rugged sound, quite unlike the upper-class British of today. In it, the R's are emphasized, not deleted. The "A" sound of words like *want* and *water* would harden until the first rhymed with *can't* and the second with *matter*. There are, of course, many other small changes like these, but the general effect is a more vigorous dialect. It has a sound we would now call "country," though it had no such connotations at the time.

This point can be very confusing to young actors. They are aware that the center of the continuing tradition of Shakespearean production has always been London. Even though there has been a great deal of exciting production work elsewhere in the world, and even though there are still fine companies and superior actors all over the world, London has been the most constant and admired production site. It is sometimes unclear why this does *not* authorize the speech style of its present preeminent citizens (or of its stages) as the "official" dialect for Renaissance British drama. The voice you use while training yourself must be your own, not because we are trying to deny the historic leadership of the London theater, but because you must first connect to *your* natural voice. (For the record, the issue of dialects is as hotly contested in London as anywhere. Received Pronunciation is a choice with political and social implications, not a given.) The initial goal is to develop the strength and flexibility of the voice, not to create a different sound for it.

For professional purposes, actors often study speech with an eye to ridding themselves of an unwanted regional dialect. To be able to turn a dialect (or, indeed, many of them) on or off is a useful skill that might widen the number of roles and productions in which you can participate, but it is absolutely not necessary and not desirable in this early stage of work. For now, *your* voice (with whatever dialect or regionalisms you may possess) is appropriate. The least acceptable alternative is to imitate "BBC British," in the hope that you will sound more authentic. Exciting performances of plays by Shakespeare and his contemporaries are regularly given in a variety of accents, including even those of speakers whose first language is not English. Use and be proud of your own voice. It is the "correct" voice for the exercises in this book.

A Voice and Body Sequence

The exercises that follow are designed in a sequence that will help you explore and develop your instrument. When you first read through the steps, you will find them quite lengthy. The instructions, however, take longer than the doing. Once you've learned the steps (in a couple of sessions), the process will become rapid. It is designed in such a way that you can work sequentially, adding new steps in subsequent sessions. In your first session, you might only do Steps 1 and 2, for example. The next time, you can repeat these and add the next three or four steps. When you have the whole sequence learned, it can be used in a slow, leisurely form as a training routine, or in a more abbreviated version as a warm-up.

There is a pattern to it that is important. Many steps begin with floor work. You will lie on your back on the floor and experience the most naturally relaxed form of the work. The instructions will then tell you to try it in later sessions sitting and, finally, standing. You can learn a lot about the free and easy operation of your instrument by experiencing the floor steps, but they can be misleadingly relaxing and pacifying. In performance preparation, you need to experience the greater demands of sitting, standing, and ultimately moving about while you practice these exercises. Choose carefully the proper level for any particular session. First attempts and training iterations should be done slowly. They should probably be done on the floor. The physical and mental relaxation of the experience is part of the benefit of the process.

In classroom explorations, in which time is more pressing, sitting and standing versions are more appropriate. Pre-performance warm-ups will go quickly, with standing and moving versions dominating.

All of these exercises should be done with sensible caution about your physical state. If you have a bad back or other physical ailment, seek some medical advice before undertaking any step. If you should feel physical pain or mental distress at any point, stop immediately. Sit down and just breathe normally for a few minutes to orient yourself before you continue any exercise.

If you experience dizziness, stop and sit immediately. These exercises can greatly increase the oxygen flow in people for whom deep breathing has been unfamiliar. You will get used to your increased lung capacity, and it is not harmful, but do not risk falling and hurting yourself. Stop as soon as you feel disoriented. Immediately (and carefully) sit down.

The following brief outline is a suggestion of how the following ten steps may be blended into an individual warm-up taking about twenty minutes. This will give you an overview. The rest of the chapter will explain each step in detail:

The Warm-up

Step 1: Breathing/Relaxing 3 minutes
Lie on your back and find your natural breath rhythm.
Clear your mind and relax.

Step 2: Releasing 2 minutes
Scan your body for tensions and release them.

Step 3: Grounding 2 minutes

Slowly and carefully get to your feet and find your grounded center.

Step 4: Problem Areas   2 minutes
In turn, do neck circles, shoulder circles, spine curls, and facial massage. End by "hugging the barrel."

Step 5: Vocal Freeing   with Step 4
Simultaneously with Step 4, gently hum while you are freeing problem areas.

Step 6: Vowels   2 minutes
Find the centered form of the *ahh, ooo,* and *eee* sounds. You will have to actively establish the connection of your center to the sound you are making. Work the range of placements and pitches as described previously.

Step 7: Consonants   3 minutes
Run through the consonant series (using the bone prop for each sound pair, and then removing it again to repeat them) to warm up and stretch all of the muscular components that will articulate these sounds.

Step 8: Words   2 minutes
Work the beginning words of an arbitrary warm-up selection, or a speech from the play for which you are warming up. Attending to the physical relaxation and centering you have accomplished so far, begin to concentrate on individual words. Work each word, one at a time, to find its sound values as well as the images it evokes.

Step 9: Phrases   2 minutes
Shift from words to phrases, again concentrating on meaningful patterns of sound as well as content. Notice that as you get further into head work, bodily relaxation and centered breathing can fade away. Keep focusing these elements as you speak.

Step 10: Lines   2 minutes
Finish with speaking in lines while walking about. If you are preparing for a performance, use this time to find the proper energy level for what you have to do. The object is to be free of unnecessary tensions, with a strong voice and body connection. Be cautious about doing the work so leisurely that you are not ready to go on. Instead, finish out with a few lines that are spoken at full volume while you are walking at full speed. Gear up.

Step I: Breath and Relaxation

The fundamental level of all voice and body work lies in the breath. Breathing is natural and easy until the tensions of everyday life (and, of course, the additional effect of stage fright) interfere with the process.

For the actor, the first step is simply to reexperience free, relaxing breathing. Begin your work, then, with exercises that will help you feel this simple, natural state.

---

breathing/relaxation exercises

---

1.   Lie on the floor on your back. Bend your legs at the knees so that your (shoeless) feet sit flat on the floor. Consciously think to yourself that you want to let your back spread widely across the floor, especially at the shoulders, and you want to let your spine lengthen. Don't "flatten" the small of your back, but let it relax until it eases toward the floor, getting your back as flat as possible.

Consciously relax your neck, your shoulder joints, your elbows, and your wrists. Flop one hand over on the diaphragm and let the hand just lie there unsupported. Your other arm is on the floor. It helps to spread your elbows away from the body.

Just lie there and experience your breathing. For two minutes do nothing but let the natural rise and fall of your breath entertain and fascinate you. Let all your air out with each breath, and then just wait patiently. Don't "take a breath," but just watch as an unattached observer as your body does what comes naturally. Notice the natural (and not consciously directed) process of breathing. The hand on your diaphragm will feel the small, involuntary movement that initiates the taking of the breath. Register it, but don't do anything about it; just breathe.

2.   Still on the floor, breathe in through your nose and then sigh out through your mouth slowly and silently, while counting to ten in your head. Let any remaining air out, but resist breathing in. Wait for a silent count of five. Feel your body prepare for the incoming breath. Notice, in fact, its insistence! After the five-count, don't consciously draw breath in, but just stop resisting it. Notice what it is like for your body to draw in this full breath automatically. Where does the air go? Pay attention to where your body expands as it fills.

It is likely not the upper chest, where most of us think we breathe, but lower—behind the lower ribs and even down into the stomach.

3.   After getting up slowly, sit in a chair and continue this exercise. Sit with your back straight and flat, neither slumping nor sway-backed. Just breathe naturally. Notice the sensation of breathing in this position. Compare this to the easy, free breathing you experienced on the floor. Enjoy the pressure-free and tension-free experience of breathing. Attempt to keep your breath as natural and free of interference as you felt on the floor. After a minute or two of this, begin to breathe in the pattern in which you sigh out on a (silent) ten-count, resist breathing in for a five-count, and finally allow a new breath to fall in.

4.   After slowly standing, continue the experience of breathing in an easy, natural rhythm. Can you keep the same tension-free breath you previously felt? If not, where are the tensions that are limiting your breath? After a few iterations, breathe in on a three-count, out on a ten-count, resist for five, and let a new breath fall in. (Few of us, by the way, can keep our breathing free, at first, while standing. It takes time to begin to notice where and how we interfere by adding unneeded tension. Give yourself time to learn the process. Repeat this exercise daily, and notice how much better you get at monitoring and releasing unnecessary tension over time.)

Step 2: Releasing
Once you have developed your breathing and used it to relax, you can move onto the more advanced concern of releasing excess tension. In this step, you will be monitoring your body for stored tension and releasing it. The main part of this exercise is mental. You will be scanning your body for physical signs of tension and releasing it, but it is your mental ability to *detect* tension that is being developed.

releasing exercises

1.   On your back on the floor, imagine that you are one of those pieces of medical equipment that scans the body in millimeter slices. Start your scan at the bottoms of your feet and begin sweeping it up

toward your head. Along the way, monitor the state of relaxation of each body part as the scan passes over it. Take about two minutes to go over the entire body. Notice where your main tensions lie.

2. Now go back again and tense as tightly as you can all the muscles in the left side of your body as the scan passes over it, taking about thirty seconds to do the complete pass. Scrunch your left foot up tightly, with your toes curled down toward its center. Flex your left ankle. Tense your calf and then your thigh. Continue up your body, taking special care to see that your arm, wrist, and fingers tighten. Tense the shoulder, the neck, and the left side of your face. Can you do it without tensing the right side? Notice the difference? Are there places on your right side that feel just as tense as the left? Can you let the right side relax while your left tenses?

3. Now pass the scan up again and relax the left side as you tense the right. Compare and contrast constantly.

4. Passing the scan up one more time, tense the whole body as tightly as possible, and then, just as the scanner passes the last millimeter of your body, all at once let it just release into a state of total passivity. Try to let the muscles do nothing. Only the floor is holding you up.

5. Remember: the main point is mental. Can you detect and release tension? Train yourself over time to do this whether on the floor, sitting, standing, or moving.

Step 3: Getting Grounded

For the first few times through the exercise sequence, this step may be experienced lying down, with your whole back acting as the contact point, but it is primarily intended to be done standing. When doing it in the floor work form, you will be abbreviating this step.

If (in later iterations) you are making a transition from floor work, come to your feet very slowly. You may be a bit dizzy. Get to your feet in slow stages. First sit up, then kneel, then slowly come to a full stand. There is no rush.

the grounded position

The point of what you are about to do is find your center and connect it firmly with the earth.

1.   Stand with your feet directly under your shoulders and hips. Your stance should not be too wide nor (more commonly) too narrow. Put your weight just slightly on the balls of your feet. Make sure your knees are not locked.

2.   Think of your legs as the connection between your innermost self and the ground. Imagine them as conduits that lend the strength of the earth to you. They are not dead statues, but energy cables.

3.   Very gently rock forward and back, then side to side. If you can do this without feeling off balance or out of kilter, you are centered. If you feel at any point that you are losing your balance, it means that something is unduly tense or that your balance is not invested in your center. Check especially your jaw and your shoulders, which are the two most common culprits. (If you cannot achieve a centering on the first try, don't despair. Our next major step will help you correct problems, and perhaps you will get it next time.)

4.   Focus your eyes straight ahead, on the horizon. Think that all the space you see is under your control. You are connected to it all through your contact with the ground.

Step 4: Working Out Problems
Nearly everyone has a few chronic trouble spots, which are frequently found in just a few areas. The short sequence that follows is to help you check the usual suspects and correct them. If you are among the lucky few who don't experience any tension in these areas, don't worry that you are hurting these areas. The exercises will just help keep you loose.

problem area exercises

1a.   If you are lying on the floor, just let your head fall to the left until your cheek is on or near the floor and you are looking at the wall to your left along the floor line. Gently roll your cheek to the right so that it is near the floor and you are looking right. Roll back and forth easily between the two.

1b. In sitting or standing versions, just quit holding your head up and let it fall straight forward until your chin is sitting on your chest. Slowly begin to roll your head to your left so that your left ear is sitting directly over your left shoulder. Keep rolling backward so that you find yourself looking straight up. Keep rolling around the circle so that your right ear passes over your right shoulder, and finally your head is back in the center again. This is all done slowly. (Be especially aware of possible dizziness with this exercise. The first time you try it, you may want a spotter who just stands by to correct your balance. You can trade places with this person to return the favor.) Go around the circle a couple of times; then reverse direction. Try not to tense your shoulder up to meet your ear, but let your neck relax down to allow your ear to meet your shoulder.

2a. On the floor, hunch your shoulders up toward your ears, and then lower them again several times to loosen them up.

2b. In standing and sitting versions, roll your shoulders in circles, forward as far as they will go, then up toward your ears, backward as far as possible, and then let them drop heavily to your sides. Take a deep breath and as you exhale see if you can drop them further. It is not uncommon for first timers to end with their shoulders four or five inches lower at the end than when they started.

3a. On the floor, gently roll up your spine to a sitting position. Imagine that your spine is a long line of blocks. Just lift the first one connecting to your head, then the one next to it, then the one next to it. Use this one-at-a-time process to lift your spine an inch at a time off the floor. (If you have experienced back problems in the past, do this exercise with caution.) Slowly build your stack of blocks up until the line of blocks that was lying on the floor is now sitting vertically. Don't let your neck and shoulders tense up again while you do this exercise. Gently roll down the spine again until you are again lying on the floor.

3b. From a sitting or standing position, where the spine is already vertical, roll *down* the spine. You will end bent over from the waist. Keep your knees unlocked. You are not bending over like an ironing board being lowered into position, but are letting your head drop against your chest and letting your back follow one vertebra at a time. Once you are all the way upside down, reverse the process and roll up again. Keep your neck and shoulders loose. When you are upside down, your arms will just dangle over toward the floor, possibly touching your feet if you are flexible.

4.   Whether you are on the floor or standing, scrunch your face up like a prune, as tightly as you can. Next, stretch it to the opposite extreme, with your eyes open as wide as possible and your mouth open in a big yawn. Alternate quickly. With your hands, reach up and take hold of your chin. Give up all muscular control of your jaw. Go slack-jawed and then shake your jaw with your hands. Vibrate it loose. With the heels of your hands, dig into the jaw muscles just under the ears and stroke downward, massaging away the tension you find there.

5.   Either lying on the floor or standing, end this sequence by centering yourself again and then imagining there is a barrel in front of you. Reach out in a wide circle and hug the barrel. Your arms will make a large round circle, and your body will curve to accommodate the barrel's bulge. While hugging the barrel, take a deep breath and let your back spread out horizontally to give you an extra couple of inches of reach around the barrel. Keep your neck, shoulders, and spine loose as you do this. Check to see if you are making faces. Don't tense up your face again. Your whole body should be working in harmony.

Step 5: Vocal Freeing
Once you have done the bodily warm-up, you can move on to some light vocal freeing. This is accomplished in the simplest manner imaginable.

---

humming

While lying on your back, or later sitting and standing, take a breath and then gently hum (at slightly higher than your normal speaking pitch) for the entire length of time it takes you until you run out of air. Do it again. And again. Hum one last time while you gently vibrate your whole body to shake loose. Each hum should be just loud enough to be heard by someone standing three feet in front of you, and it should last about fifteen to twenty seconds.

Step 6: Exploring Sound

Once in touch with your breath again, you are ready to begin the process of exploring sound. We learned to combine speech into sound so long ago, most of us have lost all connection with the wonder of the many separate sounds that make up our words. In a leisurely exploration, take time now to reexplore all of the individual sounds in your repertoire. In the exercises that follow, you will begin with the simplest, most direct sounds you can make, go on to a more specific examination of vowels, and finally add consonants.

---

vowel sound exercises

---

1.   Lie on the floor (as in the breathing exercises) and again establish your natural breathing pattern. After clearing your mind of any clutter, draw in your breath. Think of this breath as a deep sigh of relaxation and contentment. Breathe out on a silent ten-count. Wait for a count of five and draw breath again. This time, as you breathe out, put a lip lightly in front of your teeth and let a little *ffff* sound form. Let the sound last the whole length of your ten-counts while you breathe out. In the next iteration, "allow" a light and easy *ahhh* sound to form. Don't force it; just let it form naturally. Think of this sound as if it were starting underneath your hand and flowing unimpeded up a great open channel, through your spacious throat and out your gloriously wide mouth. It is not the slightly nasal sound we make when warning children not to be naughty, but the sound of contentment that escapes us during the perfect massage! Let it last until you are out of breath.

2.   Repeat this sound until you can feel it begin from your very center and it creates a sensation of release and relaxation. This exercise may last five or more minutes the first time you try it. Enjoy making this sound again and again. Then switch to the *oooo* sound, as in the word *loose*. This is the sound we use to express pleasure. Just making this sound ought to feel good! Try it several times, each time making the sound last the length of your release of breath.

3. Finally, make the *eeee* sound, as in *free*. Make this sound last also. It will vibrate your sinuses and facial muscles until they tickle! Try it several times. The third or fourth time you try it, start on a high pitch and let it swoop down through your full range as you release your breath, like the sound of a child makes while coming down a slide toward you.

4. Now on three successive breaths, try all three sounds starting with *ahhh*, moving to *oooo*, and ending with *eeee*. On subsequent days, try the many vowels that lie between these sounds, like the vowels in *hook, cold, dawn, hot, loud, coin, lung, burn, bad, let, face, ink, lie, hear,* and *air*. Try them all on many pitches, from high in your "falsetto" or head voice all the way down to a chest-rattling low note.

For every vowel you try, keep the sense of connection to the impulse that begins sound in your center and to the sense of openness and freedom. Never force the sound, but allow full, easy expression.

On another day, repeat the same exercise while sitting. On yet another day, repeat the exercise while standing.

Step 7: Consonants

Vowels create the music of speech, but the form and vigor of it come from consonants. There are far more consonants than vowels. They are difficult at first to think about in detail, because such small muscular movements create such great variety.

As an aid to learning about consonants by feel, you are going to use a "bone prop" to hold your teeth slightly apart. This will exaggerate the movements of your articulators just a little, making them easier to feel. Bone props are small props between a half-inch and three-quarters inch in length. The best professional varieties of these are made of a plastic that resembles bone in color and texture. They are shaped like a small length of a pencil, with notches in the top and bottom. These are placed between the teeth in the front center of the mouth.

For our purposes, you won't need a professional variety. A cork or a small section of a dowel will work. A cut-down wooden coffee stirrer from your local coffee bar is ideal. Start with a half-inch length and test it for comfort. It should hold your jaws apart and steady but not so wide that you gag or feel extreme jaw tension. A good fit is a personal matter, but seven-eighths of an inch is the absolute maximum.

This exercise will be done sitting up at first and later, standing. If you have been doing floor work to this point, get up slowly and carefully. Eventually this step can be done without the prop, but continue to use it for at least a month, so you really learn the articulation series. Make yourself a prop, and then go to work on the following exercises:

consonant exercises

1. Sitting in front of a mirror so you can observe the movements of your lips, tongue, and other articulators, make and repeat the following pairs of sounds seven or eight times.

First *p,* then *b.* Don't say the letter name, but make the sound associated with it. This first pair will require much more lip effort than usual because the bone prop is holding your teeth apart. This is precisely the point. Concentrate both on what you see and on what you feel. Notice that these are the same sounds in unvoiced (p) and voiced (b) form. Learn from this experience exactly how this set of sounds is produced.

Including the first pair, here is the whole series:

p–b
f–v
s–z
k–g
t–d
th (as in **th**ick)–th (as in **th**ee)
sh–zh (as in **Z**sa-Zsa)
ch–dj (as in the end of ju**dg**e)

Now look at this additional series of unpaired consonants:

m
n
r
l
w

Make each of the sounds several times, feeling and looking carefully. This exercise is tiring. It takes a great deal of energy, especially with the bone prop in place. This is a wonderful analogy for the amount of vocal energy required for performance, however. In our mumbling modern age, we may vastly underestimate the amount of simple effort that goes into a rhetorical performance.

2. Pick a sonnet (any one will do, but number 12 works well for this) and read it aloud. Then read just the first four lines again with the bone prop in your mouth. Go very slowly, but try to make yourself understood. Immediately remove the bone prop and read the whole sonnet again, trying to keep the sensation of the effort and precision you used when you had the bone prop in your mouth. If there is anyone with you, ask them if there was any difference in the quality of the first and last reading. What differences do you notice?

3. Using a sonnet or a few lines of a monologue, speak the lines, breaking them down into each individual sound. Take a line like the first sentence of *Merchant of Venice,* "In sooth, I know not why I am so sad," and take it apart literally sound by sound: iiiiiiiiiiiiiiiii nnnnnnnnnnnnnnn/sssssssssssss ooooooooo thhhhh, IIIIIIIIIIIIIIIIIIIIIIIIIIIIIII/knnnnnnnnnnnnnnnnnnnnnn ooooooooooow/nnnnnnnnnnnnnn oooooooooooooooooo tttt/ whhhhhhhhhh yyyyyyyyyyyyyyyyyyyyyyy/IIIIIIIIIIIIIIIIIIIIIIIII/ aaaaaaaaaaaaaammmmmmmmmm/sssssssssssssssss ooooooooooo/ sssssssssssssssss aaaaaaaaaaaaaaaaaaaaaa dddd. Break it apart to the point that it feels ridiculously slow. Enjoy the sound of each individual phonetic unit. Revel in the repetition of the "s" sound. Spend ten or more seconds on each sound. The line may take you a couple of minutes to explore. The point of this whole series of exercises is to rediscover the simplicity and joy of pure sound combinations.

Step 8: Sound into Words

From discrete sounds, we want to begin to use words selectively and carefully. Each word is individually precious and meaningful. Using the same sonnet as in the last step, you are going to do some work on the individual words in it.

word exercises

1. If you are working in a group, form a circle and read the sonnet aloud one word at a time. Each person in the circle will read just one word before the person next to him takes over. Continue around the circle until the sonnet is complete. If you are working alone, take just the first quatrain (four lines) and speak the sonnet one word at a time. Give each and every word equal weight and attention.

2. In the group exercise, read the sonnet again, but this time the person next to you can either say the next word or (if they feel you rushed your word or were inattentive to it) say the single word *no*. If you hear the word *no*, say your word again. Don't just say it louder or slower, say it with greater attention and relish. The next person in line can again opt to say the next word or again say *no*. Continue until the sonnet is complete.

If you are not working with a group, see if you can find a helper/ listener. Ask this person to listen to the individual words of your quatrain. After every word, she is to say *yes* if she heard the word clearly and it was invested with full meaning, or *no* if it was in any way lesser. It is surprising how even a completely nontheatrical person can hear and detect the quality of individual words with no more instruction than this.

3. In future warm-up interactions, you can do this work yourself, taking whatever speeches you are working on and attending to them word by word. This is pointless, of course, if you are not carefully weighing and considering each word as you speak it. The whole notion here is to take the time and care to really examine each word for both its form and its content. You cannot rush it. This step is just a tiny increment above the last bit of sound work you did, when you were breaking a word apart into each component sound. The attention now is on the whole word, not its individual sounds, but it is still very detailed work.

4. In group work, try the following quick game to help focus on words, their size, and their energy. Form a circle and choose someone to be *it*. Starting with that person, go around the circle once, speaking your own name loudly and clearly for everyone to hear. *It* will then point to one person in the group, say his name and

follow it up by counting to ten. (*It* is saying, therefore, "James, one, two, three, four, five, six, seven, eight, nine, ten.) The object is to reach the count of ten before James can call another name out and begin his count. The object for James is to point to someone else in the group, call her name, and begin counting before *it* reaches ten. If James succeeds, the game continues. If he fails, he must sit down. The game continues until there are only two final players.

Once your group has played the game a few times, and everyone's name is familiar, try a variation in which the name calling and counting should take exactly ten syllables. Thus, if the person you are calling on has a one-syllable name, the counting would sound like this: "Jane, two, three, four, five, six, sev'n, eight, nine, ten." If the person has a two -syllable name, it would go: "Eric, three, four, five, six, sev'n, eight, nine, ten." This can go to any length name, thus: "Latawnia, five, six, sev'n, eight, nine, ten." You can only put someone out by getting the name called, the syllable count right, and the count completed before he can call another name.

Step 9: Phrases

From attending to words (their form, their structure, their meaning, their length), we want to look at the shortest possible units of combined meaning—the phrase. We will again work with our sonnet, or (if you wish) a speech you may currently be preparing. The emphasis will shift now to short combinations of words.

---

phrase exercises

---

1. Again in your group circle, read the sonnet with each person reading until she encounters a punctuation mark. (It is important that everyone in the group be looking at the same edition of the sonnet when trying this. For reasons explained later in the book, punctuation can vary greatly from edition to edition.) As in the earlier word exercise, the next speaker can read his phrase or say *no*. If the response is *no*, the first speaker should repeat the phrase. Continue working this way until the sonnet is complete.

If you are working without the benefit of a group, or if you are warming-up individually, speak the sonnet one phrase at a time, stopping after each phrase. Repeat each phrase several times before moving to the next.

Whether working in the group or alone, the object is not to listen to yourself, but to attend to the combined effect of the words. Think about what this combination of words means together that the individual words do not mean alone. This may be because the combination produces a new sense. In the third line of Sonnet 12, "When I behold the violet past prime," the last three words mean something quite different when taken together than they each mean individually. It may also be that the juxtaposition of sounds adds to meaning. "Past prime," has a repeated sound that binds the phrase more tightly.

2.   Working individually, walk as you speak each phrase. Continue in a natural flow with the piece, but change directions sharply with each new phrase, which, of course, should be corresponding to new thoughts. Try walking in square patterns, triangular patterns, and assorted other geometric shapes. Notice how the lengths of phrases dictate different shapes as you walk. Speak the sonnet in normal time, marking the phrases by executing sharp, almost military, turns.

Step 10: Lines
From phrases, we want to look at another way of organizing units of meaning, which is the line. This step may produce surprising results.

---
line exercise
---

1.   Once again working in the group circle, read the sonnet with each speaker taking one line. Notice the places that phrases (as you discovered them in the last exercise) are split across lines. Read the sonnet as a group so that it makes sense. This may mean that two successive speakers must work closely together to keep a phrase flowing across a line break. Don't apply a vocal pattern that implies you are at the end of the phrase just because you are at the end of the line you will be speaking. Only use the kinds of vocal patterns we apply to bring closure to a thought if your line end is also the end of the phrase.

If working alone, try reading the sonnet as you did previously, with sharp direction changes at the ends of phrases. This time, also stop and kick *on* the last word of each line. (Watch the tendency to say the word and then kick. Instead, kick *as* you say it.) If the line and phrase end simultaneously, you'll be doing a kick and a turn at the same time! Don't worry, you can do it. It only sounds hard. In your warm-up you'll find that it is fun.

Summary

This is the end of the voice/body series. Each individual step could be used for a full hour's worth of exploratory work in early training. Later, each step can be speeded considerably into a warm-up routine.

Further Reading

If you want to know more about this subject, I recommend the following readings. Each of the three authors cited below have written a pair of books. The subject of the first is the voice, with the second work concentrating on text work. Though all are good, I am slightly inclined toward the newest of these by Rodenburg, because her bright feminist arguments illuminate the manner in which voice work is also personal empowerment.

Berry, Cicely. 1974. *Voice and the Actor*. 1st American ed. New York: Macmillan.

————. 1992.*The Actor and the Text*. rev. ed. New York: Applause Books.

Linklater, Kristin. 1975. *Freeing the Natural Voice*. New York: Drama Book Specialists.

————. 1992. *Freeing Shakespeare's Voice*. New York: Theater Communications Group.

Rodenburg, Patsy. 1992. *The Right to Speak*. New York: Routledge.

————. 1993. *The Need for Words: Voice and the Text*. New York: Routledge.

5 Fusing Passion and Eloquence: Sonnets

Though Shakespeare is best known to theater students as a playwright, he is also the author of 154 sonnets (plus some miscellaneous extras that were incorporated into plays) that are extremely useful as beginning exercises for classical actors. We will be looking at these in this exercise to help us learn the fundamental lesson of classical acting: fusing passion and eloquence. The modern tendency is to act between the lines (say a few words and then pause to let the emotion catch up) or, alternatively, act beneath the lines (say the lines in an emotionally controlled way to imply there are powerful emotions being suppressed). The challenge, and the joy, of the plays of Shakespeare and his contemporaries is acting *on* the line.

This is easily said, but not automatically easy to do. The words do not have intensity all by themselves. Though the subject matter of the sonnets is both deep and profound, it is possible (indeed, common) to read them boringly. Smearing one big, emotionally indulgent performance over them won't help either. The sonnets are not just about emotion, but emotion *intelligently expressed*. To encompass the passion of the sonnets, the actor must also master their eloquence. The following exercise will help us learn to do both.

Why Start with Sonnets?

Though the sonnets are nondramatic material, they are superb for beginning acting exercises. For our starting place, sonnets have several advantages over dramatic speeches. Foremost, they have a concentrated form of fourteen lines, which sets useful limits on the size of the task. Each is a self-contained little package, complete in itself. For this reason, there is less distraction of the kind that arises about questions of character and interpretation when using extracted speeches. A final point is that the sonnets all develop emotionally, frequently with a reversal or twist in the last lines, so you learn not to swamp a speech with one generalized emotion. From the sonnets you can learn how to handle verse and rhetorical arguments in neat, small packages, with the added fun of exploring their extremely intriguing subject matter. "Just by speaking them and feeling them on the tongue, we make ourselves more easy with the rhythm of the language and how to manage it," says world-famous voice teacher Cicely Berry.[1]

What Are Sonnets About?

The sonnets are all written to, or about, an exceptionally striking young man or a dark-featured woman, or (in a few notorious cases) both. As a character inside the sonnets, the poet himself has a distinct voice and personality, but we do not know if this is a fictional pose or Shakespeare's authentic voice. In either case, you will find yourself adopting the attitudes and viewpoints of the poet while speaking his words. Cicely Berry, the voice coach of the Royal Shakespeare Company, comments (in *The Actor and the Text*) that she thinks the poet's personality is usually distinctly male enough to make it slightly harder for women to enter into the sonnets with the same ease and identification as men. For the example given in this chapter, great care has gone into selecting a gender-neutral sonnet to help alleviate this problem. There are, by the way, several others that share this quality that are available for individual work if gender identification is presenting difficulties.

What Is a Sonnet?

The term *sonnet* derives from the same root as the word *sonic,* having to do with sound. It literally means "little sound" and carries some of the same connotations we associate with the much more modern term *sound bite.* The sonnet is a pithy little statement in poetic form, which is memorable because it engages intense emotions. Though different poets deploy slightly different forms of the sonnet, Shakespeare's are quite consistent. As he writes them, they consist of fourteen lines of iambic pentameter, which is the same meter used throughout the plays in the blank verse.

Shakespearean sonnets consist of four distinct sections. The first four lines form a quatrain in which the first and third lines rhyme with each other, as do the second and fourth. (This rhyme scheme is notated as ABAB.) The second four lines form another quatrain employing the same pattern of rhyme, but these lines do not rhyme with the first four. (These are notated as CDCD.) The third section is another quatrain. (As you can probably predict the notation is EFEF.) The fourth and final section of the poem is composed of two lines that rhyme with each other. (This is called a couplet and is notated as GG.) The complete form looks, then, like this:

ABAB
CDCD
EFEF
GG

The trademark of the sonnet form is that in this short space the author finds a combination of intellectual argument and emotion. Shakespeare's sonnets are often about extremely intellectual concepts, such as the fleetingness of fame or the nature of human devotion, but this is expressed in ways that can only be described as extravagantly emotional. The sonnets are not soft and "poetic," not mushy, not nearly so romantic as generally assumed. They sometimes swing wildly from one emotion to another, but they don't do so in the vaguely dazed way that became associated with poets in the nineteenth century. They are vital, even aggressive. It is a mistake, I think, to approach them too seriously. They are often ironically humorous and, at the very least, clever.

Each sonnet is a structured argument. The first quatrain states a theme. The second expands on it. The third usually, but not always, personalizes it. The most common function of the third quatrain is to make a connection between the listener and the theme. The final couplet is most often a surprise twist. Sometimes it contains a complete reversal of the previous direction, or sometimes a witty comment on the theme. Occasionally it offers sudden new applications of the theme as stated.

In the abstract, this may be a bit hard to grasp, so an example is in order. Look for a minute at Sonnet 12.

Sonnet 12

When I do count the clock that tells the time	
And see the brave day sunk in hideous night;	
When I behold the violet past prime	
and sable curls [en]silvered o'er with white;	4
When lofty trees I see barren of leaves,	
Which erst from heat did canopy the herd,	
And summer's green all girded up in sheaves	
Borne on the bier with white and bristly beard:	8
Then of thy beauty do I question make	
That thou among the wastes of time must go,	
Since sweets and beauties do themselves forsake,	
And die as fast as they see others grow;	12
And nothing 'gainst time's scythe can make defense	
Save breed, to brave him when he takes thee hence.	14

Here it is easy to see the pattern. The first four lines all concern themselves with the passage of time in steadily increasing intervals: first minutes, then days, then seasons, and, finally, lifetimes. The first quatrain announces the general topic of time passing.

The second quatrain makes this more specific by citing examples from nature of things growing old.

The third quatrain suddenly turns the subject to the very personal matter of how it is inevitable that the hearer will age also. His/her beauty is also bound to fade.

The first twelve lines tell us that everything ages and dies, ourselves included. Even adding the next line of the poem, which says that there is nothing we can do about it, we still do not yet know the point of the whole thing. The very last line springs a suprise on us. It tells us that there is something we can do to defeat time. We can breed. (In this context, *breed* is not a verb, but a noun meaning "children," but it is only slightly less shocking with this caveat.)

If, for some reason, the last line of this poem were lost, we would think of it entirely differently. Up until the very last line, the point seems to be something like, "Accept your mortality." This is not a slight subject, not at all ridiculous in and of itself. With the last line, however, we get the clever twist that helps us see all that has gone before in a different light. It is suddenly emotionally loaded in a very different way.

If you think for a minute what young person you would have the audacity to give this advice to, you will realize that this is an extremely personal matter. I remember, shortly after I was married, people who would ask me if my wife and I were planning to have children. I thought then (and think now) that it was an awfully intrusive question. To go a step further and mention that it might be a good idea, since I'm going to die and leave nothing behind if I don't, is well beyond the question.

It is an outrageous poem, really, not the sedate lines we sometimes stereotype poetry as being. It is exciting, a bit cheeky, shocking. It is effective because the most in-your-face matters are left until the last second and then sprung with such ingenuity that you almost burst out laughing at the brazenness of it.

You can see, then, why sonnets make such popular material for actors. The textual matters are contained within a brief enough space that they can be considered without becoming overwhelming. The subject matter is deeply thoughtful, but the approach is so daring that it is thrilling.

sonnet exercise

Now that you know a bit about the form and nature of sonnets, it is time to go to work on one. At the end of the following instructions, Sonnet 94 will be analyzed, but you may work on any sonnet of your choosing. Our example is here as a reference point for the ensuing discussion.

Step 1: Preparatory Work. In the first stage, you are just getting yourself ready. Pick a sonnet and read it *aloud* several times. Just enjoy it as poetry.

Once you have had time to live with your sonnet for a while, see if you can paraphrase the argument. This can be very brief and pithy. (For Sonnet 12 we might say, "Like everything else, you are going to die, so in order to leave something behind, have kids.") Don't be surprised if it doesn't sound at all poetic any more. This is done just to be sure you understand the point.

Next, look at the accumulated images, which may not have much to do directly with the theme. The word pictures of Sonnet 12 are about spring, flowers, and nature, as well as more traditional images of death.

Step 2: Speak to Someone. Next, speak the sonnet aloud again, addressing someone. Think of someone that you could actually imagine yourself saying this to, and *meaning* it. Say the sonnet aloud, and speak *to* the person about which you are thinking. Don't just read the poem. (In partner or group work, actually speak to someone in the room and *mean* what you say—no polite fictions that this is just an exercise.) Try to imagine what steps you would have to take to make this socially acceptable. Think about how the person you are addressing will respond. What is her reaction to you being so far into her business? Notice the emotional involvement that arises from direct address. Notice also that the words have a multiplicity of possibilities. There is a vast range of ways that the words can be said and meant. Think of a new person, or change partners, and notice how the words come out differently. A different approach is called for with a different person.

This is the heart of the sonnet exercise. The goal here is to learn to use the eloquent language to find the passion of the piece. Don't settle for a smooth surface reading, but dig in to discover the excitement of creating emotional intensity *through* language.

Step 3: Verbal Conceits. Say the sonnet again, looking especially at the interesting verbal aspects. Is there any antithesis built into the piece? If so, emphasize it. Look for alliteration and assonance. See if you can make them more apparent as you again speak the words. Jokes? Puns? Say your sonnet again and be outrageous with the wit. Use the devices to further your exploration of the passion.

Step 4: Scansion. Take a moment with your poem and scan it. Look hard at the rhythms. Be sure you understand them. Are there any tricky bits? Consult footnotes in your edition or an expert, such as your teacher, if you need help. Once you think you have it in hand, read it again for the steadiness of the beat. With each line, build to the last word. (One way to train yourself to do this is to kick or punch the air as you say the last word of each line. Notice the extra life and energy you get!) Don't break it up too much. See what happens if you read it not as fourteen lines, but as one long thought. (Think again of song. A musician wouldn't play one good phrase, then take a break to savor it, waiting to start again until he felt ready. He would honor the form of the whole song. So should you.)

Step 5: Experimentation. Now, whisper your sonnet. Still keeping the beat, feel the intensity and urgency. Whisper to someone far away from you. Try to make yourself understood even across a large space. Switch then to a new tack: speak your sonnet varying the tone. Go as lightly as possible to see what this stirs up. Fast. Slow. Look for humor. Take it extravagantly. Intellectually. Sing it. Find the balance point.

Step 6: Finishing Touches. Put the basic package together. Try your sonnet, keeping the best of all your discoveries. The one thing of which you should be especially cognizant is pace. If you imagined the most lugubrious pace possible as a one, and the fastest speed that you could still speak clearly as a ten, you are probably speaking now at a four or five. Speed it up to a six or seven and see how that feels. If it feels just a little too fast, just slightly out of your control, then it is right. Our comfort zone is too slow for Shakespearean performance. (In modern speech, we speak at the equivalent of 700 iambic pentameter lines per hour, but most actors find Shakespeare works best at 1000 lines per hour.) Speed up just until you feel you are on the edge of too fast. Your listeners will feel the excitement and urgency. You are then ready to present the sonnet to someone.

An Example Sonnet Exercise

Sonnet 94

They that have power to hurt, and will do none
That do not do the thing they most do show

Who moving others, are themselves as stone
Unmoved, cold, and to temptation slow,   4
They rightly do inherit heaven's graces
And husband nature's riches from expense;
They are the lords and owners of their faces,
Others but stewards of their excellence.   8
The summer's flower is to the summer sweet,
Though to itself it only live and die
But if that flower with base infection meet,
The basest weed outbraves his dignity: 12
For sweetest things turn sourest by their deeds
Lilies that fester smell far worse than weeds.   14

1. Opening variation, pow'r 3. Stone is an historic rhyme. 4. unmovéd
5. End variation 7. End variation 8. Opening variation 9. flow'r 11.
flow'r 12. Dignity is an historic rhyme. 14. Opening variation.

Step 1: Preparatory Work. Sonnet 94 is among the more complex of the sonnets because of its ambivalent tone. It begins by praising those that resist the temptation to abuse their power. The second quatrain expands this to imply that they are even more praiseworthy for knowing themselves, because they actively resist a potential to harm others as opposed to passively being kind because they are unaware of their power. The third quatrain introduces a botanical metaphor, which says that even the isolated, unpollinated flower is sweet to the summer, but watch out, because it is extra susceptible to infection that will leave it worse than the common weed. There is a distinct change of direction in the couplet, because we are now talking about the good turning actively bad. The sonnet finishes with an extremely memorable line, which makes the point explicit. One reading of this sonnet might go something like, "Goodness is nice, but only if it is arrived at as a choice. The passively good are prone to spectacular falls." I tend to read it even more personally. I'd paraphrase it, "You are good to me, but I doubt you know your power over me. I'm afraid you'll turn on me." The emotion of the sonnet comes through the ambiguity of the poet's point. It all sounds like praise for a long time, but it then slips suddenly into criticism in the couplet. The sonnet is full of examples of things that sound bad, which turn out to be good, like "unmovéd, cold," which are repellent qualities until they resolve "to temptation slow," which is an admirable quality. The effect is to portray an auditor whose goodness the poet likes but does not trust.

The poet is having trouble telling the difference between the attractive sides of the object and its bad sides. (Ever felt like this in real life?) Like Sonnet 12, this one employs botanical imagery. It also uses images of farming in the second quatrain.

Step 2: Direct Address. More than most sonnets, this one has a variable quality that makes it fascinating. A whole class can work on it and every person find a distinct reading, depending on whom they address. The degrees of liking and simultaneously distrusting the goodness of the listener can balance at many points along the scale. In this sonnet, there is little black and white, but all sorts of shades of gray. The author is saying something powerfully, but indirectly.

Step 3: Verbal Conceits. This piece is built around antithesis, starting with a strong example in the first line. There are others in lines 2 and 3. Lines 7 and 8 offer contrasts to each other. Line 10 contains another example. Lines 11 and 12 are paired in contrast to one another. Finally, both lines of the couplet contain antitheses. At minimum, there are eight antithetical pairs in fourteen lines, certainly a high proportion. Lines 1 and 3 and lines 10 and 12 contain historic rhymes, which give them a subtle interest.

Step 4: Scansion. Immediately under the sonnet there is a set of notes on scansion keyed line by line. There are three opening variations employed in this sonnet, including the first line, which gets an extra little pulse from a strong first word, and the last line, which is rendered all the more memorable because of it. Lines 5 and 7 employ the line end variation, which always comes in pairs in sonnets because of the rhyme scheme. Both *flower* and *power* get elided down to one syllable, while *unmovéd* gets an expanded ending. All in all, however, this is a fairly regular sonnet. Its major interest does not lie in its rhythmic variations, but in its fascinating tone.

Step 5: Experimentation. This, of course, is a matter of individual work and discovery, but I have observed that this sonnet has a powerful effect when whispered intimately. The effect often produces a sense of urgent warning. Looking for the sardonic humor of the piece also occasionally produces interesting results.

Step 6: Do it and enjoy! See if you can express the strength of your feelings through the beauty of your words. The piece is about two things: passionate idea and beautiful expression. Don't let one dominate the other.

a group exercise: sonnet for a sovereign

As a follow-up to your first sonnet exercise, you may be interested in participating in a group activity suggested by Robert Barton in his book *Style for Actors*. In this exercise, a group member is selected (usually by random lottery) to play the sovereign—Queen Elizabeth or King James, as appropriate. (In some classes, your instructor will arrange for a visitor to play the role.) On the timetable decided by your group, prepare a sonnet to be presented to the sovereign. The sonnet should be memorized. For the presentation, you will present your sonnet as a part of a courtly ritual, in which you will try to demonstrate your facility with language, your devotion to your monarch, and your wit, cleverness, and charm. Afterward, you'll discuss what it felt like to honor and be honored. See what can you learn about patronage from this exercise.

Below is a more elaborate set of instructions I have given a group that might be helpful as you prepare for a visit from the Queen.

1. Rise when Her Majesty is announced, bow when She enters the room, and remain bowing until She is seated. Remain standing until instructed to do otherwise. Prepare for the possibility that Her Majesty will not ever have you sit. She has been known to keep the court standing for hours at a time.

2. No order of presentation will be set, as Her Majesty may well choose from among her subjects according to Her whim. When your opportunity arises, step forward to share the platform, bow again, and introduce yourself in a loud, confident voice.

3. You may feel free to talk to Her Majesty, especially if addressed. You may address Her as "Your Majesty" or "Most Gracious Sovereign" or even imaginative titles, such as "Superb Gloriana," but do not be overly casual. Under no circumstances address Her by Her given name. Her Majesty is the most powerful woman, and arguably person, in the world. No title, no compliment will seem unwarranted.

Figure 2. "Queen Elizabeth" addressing a class of students in the sonnet exercise. Dr. JoAllen Bradham, a Shakespearean scholar and author, is playing the queen. Photo by Mimi Fitipaldi. Used by permission of Kennesaw State University.

Our Sovereign likes to be complimented, even flattered. You cannot overstate your praise, but Her Majesty will not be pleased if you underplay it.

Two quick asides:

Her Majesty loves to be complimented for her beauty. Beware, however, that she is very sensitive about the subject of age. Her spirit is that of a young girl, and so she should be treated. It is common to address nobility as being young and vital, while characterizing yourself as old and decrepit, regardless of the factual situation. See Sonnets 71–77 of our beloved poet for examples of this conceit.

Her Majesty has been known to flirt outrageously with physically fit young men. She is particularly fond of a well-trained calf muscle. Flirting back is acceptable, but do not lose your head or, as the late Lord Essex discovered, you can lose your head. Her Majesty is a strong woman and appreciates her noblewomen most when they are also strong and independent.

4.   Above all, Her Majesty values love and appreciation of language. Mean every word of your sonnet, but feel free to be extravagant and passionate. Boredom is the ultimate sin at court. To be theatrically extravagant without an inner truthfulness is also frowned on.

5.   Prepare your sonnet thoroughly. Her Majesty is also appreciative of small gifts and shows of skill, like musicianship or artistic accomplishment. She is quite stylish and will be honored if you dress for the occasion. You needn't dress in period clothing, she will honor your sense of personal style, but "gimme caps" and T-shirts displease. Chewing gum is cause for execution.

Note

1. In *The Actor and His Text,* p. 240.

Further Reading

For more information about sonnets, I recommend:

Giroux, Robert. 1982. *The Book Known as Q.* New York: Vintage Books.

The book referenced in the final exercise is a fine acting text and is particularly illuminating on performing classical drama set in period:

Barton, Robert. 1993. *Style for Actors.* Mountain View, CA: Mayfield.

"Personating": Working with Speeches

he second-level task for an actor of Shakespeare and his contemporaries is to embody the character who speaks those passionately eloquent lines. In period, this was a process called by the wonderful term *personation*—literally, "making a person." We are going to learn to do that first by looking at speeches from plays.

As a starting place, perhaps we first should attend to the advice to players written by Shakespeare himself. Though familiar, it actually contains a great deal of very fresh and sound advice:

> Speak the speech, I pray you, as I pronounced it to you, trippingly on the tongue. But if you mouth it as many of our players do, I had as lief the town crier spoke my lines. Nor do not saw the air too much with your hands, thus, but use all gently. For in the very torrent, tempest, and, as I may say, whirlwind of your passion, you must acquire and beget a temperance that may give it smoothness. O, it offends me to the soul to hear a robustious, periwig-pated fellow tear a passion to tatters, to very rags, to split the ears of the groundlings, who for the most part are capable of nothing by inexplicable dumb shows and noise. I would have such a fellow whipped for o'erdoing Termagant. It out-Herods Herod. Pray you avoid it.

Be not too tame neither. But let your own discretion be your tutor. Suit the action to the word, the word to the action, with this special observance, that you o'erstep not the modesty of nature. For anything so o'erdone is from the purpose of playing, whose end, both at the first and now, was and is to hold, as t'were, the mirror up to nature, to show virtue her own feature, scorn her own image, and the very age and body of the time his form and pressure. Now this overdone, or come tardy off, though it make the unskillful laugh, cannot but make the judicious grieve; the censure of the which one must in your allowance o'erweigh a whole theater of others. O, there be players that I have seen play, and heard others praise, and that highly, not to speak it profanely, that neither having the accent of a Christian nor the gate of a Christian, pagan, nor no man, have so strutted and bellowed that I have thought some of nature's journeymen had made men, and not made them well, they imitated humanity so abominably.

And let those who play your clowns speak no more than is set down for them; for there be of them that will themselves laugh to set on some quantity of barren spectators to laugh, too, though in the mean time some necessary question of the play be then to be considered. That's villainous, and shows a most pitiful ambition in the fool that uses it. (From *Hamlet* III.ii)

Contained within the speeches of Shakespeare's plays is some of the most vital, thrilling, exhilarating, profound, hilarious, and—let's face it—daunting material imaginable for actors. Shakespeare wrote in a time in which his unbounded enthusiasm for original and inventive language was allowed free reign, as it was for his contemporaries as well. The result was that the decades leading up to and immediately following the year 1600 were arguably the peak of dramatic writing in English. The sheer number of superb selections from the plays of the period boggles the mind, and intimidates it, too. Who has not heard that Shakespeare was the *greatest* dramatist of all time? (A friend of mine once suggested that he was not just intimidated by Shakespeare's reputation as the greatest, but that all his candidates for runner-up were alive and working at the same time as Shakespeare.) It can take a good deal of *chutzpah* to tackle the task of performing this material.

In my experience as a teacher and director, I find a great deal of "ShakesFear" about attempting to perform early modern plays, or even selections from them. That is unfortunate. Of course the material has its challenges, and they can be formidable, but what makes Shakespeare and his fellows "great" is that their plays contain built-in support systems which aid the actor in reaching those heights, about which we have all heard so much. Two of the greatest writers of this period, Shakespeare and Jonson, were actors themselves and understood what performers needed from them. The approach of this chapter is to examine ways that you can tap into those aids in preparing and performing a speech from a play, be it as an audition selection, a classroom monologue, or a piece destined for public consumption. The experience will be, I believe, invigorating and exciting.

Why Speeches?

Working on extracted speeches has a lot of applications. On the simplest, most blatantly pragmatic level, monologues are the stuff of which auditions are built, and auditions are the hurdle we must all leap if we want to be cast in a play from this period.

On a higher level, work on monologues is the route to learning to meld the language with characterization. They allow us to isolate just enough of a play to work on the challenges of early modern drama, without being overwhelmed with the logistics of preparing a whole role. They let us sample bits and pieces of many different characters and plays to get to know them better. Finally, monologues are pieces that we can work on by ourselves, so they present a way for us to further our exploration of acting without having (yet) to involve other people in the early stages of our process.

Monologues, Soliloquies, and Extended Asides

Monologues are, by definition, one-person exercises. Any speech from a play of sufficient length to make it worth our while can qualify. There are literally thousands of speeches of at least ten lines in length that are extractable from Shakespeare plays and the extant plays of his contemporaries. As a practical matter, not all of these make good material, of course, but a surprisingly high percentage do. For our purposes, it helps if the speech is complete in itself. (Answers to questions, for example, are indecipherable if we don't get to hear the question as part of the presentation. Likewise speeches that function to set up some other character's answer are not particularly helpful.)

Though the word applies to any solo speech, *monologue* is often reserved for speeches extracted from surrounding dialogue (which is, therefore, aimed at another character). Many such speeches can be lifted directly out of plays, and if a little minor editing is employed to remove or reassign snippets of dialogue from other speakers, many more possibilities open up. Though the list is not anywhere near exhaustive, over three hundred suggestions for possibilities appear in Kurt Daw and Julia Matthew's *A Guide to Scenes and Monologues from Shakespeare and His Contemporaries* (Portsmouth: Heinemann, 1998).

Sometimes the term *soliloquy* is used interchangeably with *monologue*, but technically it refers to speeches where characters are on stage alone speaking to themselves or (as more and more authorities are suggesting) to the audience. Soliloquies are particularly powerful when performed as nonrealistic moments in which characters break the dramatic illusion of isolation and speak to the audience directly about their situation. They have a variety of reasons for doing so, and, therefore, their speeches may take different tones. In *Othello*, Iago shares with his audience his glee at the audacity of his plan and his shock at how easy it is to manipulate humans. Hamlet is more perplexed at his situation, and reasons it through aloud, looking for guidance from the audience, or at least confirmation that he is grasping the situation correctly. Macbeth is embarked on a wildly self-destructive course and seems to tell the audience that he knows what he is doing to reassure himself of his basic sanity, though he knows (on some level) that he is undertaking unsound steps. Viola (in *Twelfth Night*) is simply surprised by her predicament and does a "reality check" with us. "This *is* weird," she seems to say, "isn't it?" In all of these cases, soliloquies function to allow characters to reveal their private thoughts to the audience.

In performance, soliloquies look very different from monologues. The latter appear, in the context of the plays, to be sections of dialogue in which one speaker holds the floor for a particularly long time, but nothing more. Soliloquies are moments in which the performance conventions shift, and the character is able to address the audience directly. In auditions or in classes in which extracted speeches are used, this difference may be much less clear because the conventions of performing monologues without partners and presenting them directly to one's auditors blur the lines between monologues and soliloquies.

Occasionally in plays, there are odd moments that seem to occupy a place midway between monologues and soliloquies. Sometimes characters address the audience directly when other characters are present, and those other characters do not appear to notice. These moments are now called *asides*, though the term is not contemporaneous to Shakespeare, and appears only in stage directions added by editors long after the fact. Frequently, these are quick little interjections, only a line or two long, but some (like Romeo's observation of Juliet on the balcony) can go on for thirty to forty lines.

For actors completely trained in the modern theater and familiar only with its conventions, the technique of direct address may seem odd at first. As will be explored in Part III of this book, Shakespeare and his fellow actors worked on stages with considerably different basic circumstances than ours. The audience was more active and, because no variable lighting put them in the dark, more *present*. The separation we now recognize between the stage and the auditorium simply didn't exist. While conventions may have changed, the latter two categories of speeches (soliloquies and asides) still imply a knowledge of the audience and a sharing with them. The energy that radiates from actors who break the invisible barriers that normally separate them from the audience is riveting, even in contemporary performance.

A Note About Performing Soliloquies

There is much more direct address in Shakespeare and in plays by his contemporaries than is generally recognized, even by historically savvy actors. Try *any* possible soliloquy or aside with an aggressive directness first. If this seems to you and your director not to work, you can always back away from the technique. Don't mistake a feeling of strangeness for failure, however. The dramatic power of such "presentationality" may seem very unfamiliar at first. It is this oddness that makes such an impression on the audience and creates a bond between the actor and audience.

Help from Playwrights

A good speech is not just a bunch of words stretching out 'til doomsday because the playwright couldn't be briefer. Speeches by Shakespeare, Marlowe, Jonson, Dekker, Middleton, and so many others of this period, are often long. Still, they are constructed with such care and craftsmanship that they are full of aids that make them much easier to remember, to present, and to appreciate than the often shorter speeches employed in contemporary theater.

The speeches are careful rhetorical packages with a strong structure. Most have a clearly discernible beginning, middle, and end. These are packaged less rigidly than sonnets, but having worked on a sonnet, you can now recognize the format. If you take time to search out the underlying structure of the speech, you'll realize that it is thoughtfully and logically put together.

The use of metaphor, of alliteration and assonance, of rhyme, and, most especially, of antithesis may seem unnecessary flourishes at first, but note how these create little signposts along the way to mark your place in the speech and to give you a target for your next place. These devices increase the imaginative content for the audience, but they also create greater memorability for the actor. They create links from one idea to the next. (Most memory problems are not with the words that complete an idea, nor are they with the words that compose the next idea. What is usually blocked in our memories are the subtle ties connecting ideas that fall in the gaps between them.) Image strings, metaphors, and the like, hook the ideas together for us. Of course, these devices are more expressive than their undecorated prose counterparts, too. Later, we'll compare some paraphrases with original text selections that will make this point clear.

Much of the preparatory work in the exercise that follows is aimed at making you more aware of how these devices work, and the extent to which they are present in your speech. It may seem like a lot of work at first, but it is worth your time. Eventually, much of this will seem more apparent, much more quickly, and the preparation of a new sonnet, speech, or role will happen more intuitively. For now, however, I urge you to complete all of the steps provided.

Shakespeare monologue preparation[1]

Step 1: Putting the Speech in Context. Once you have chosen a speech, your first step is simply to read, for enjoyment, the entire play from which it comes. Read the whole play in one sitting, if possible. At this point, don't worry about what you are going to do with the speech or even what it means, but be sure that you understand the order of events in the play and where in them the speech you have chosen occurs. *Action: Limiting yourself to a single paragraph, write a plot summary of the play that includes specific notation of your speech's place in the bigger scheme.*

Step 2: Clarifying Meanings. Consulting the notes in several editions and other sources, clarify the meaning of any individual unfamiliar words. In addition to the work of editors, your best bet is the *Oxford English Dictionary* (OED), which lists not only the current meanings of words, but also what words meant at various stages in their histories. This can be very helpful with familiar words that may have shifted meaning since Shakespeare wrote them. If your initial understanding of a line seems implausible or odd, check the main words in it in the OED to see if that changes your understanding. *Action: Write down your five best discoveries from this step, carefully noting the source consulted for the information.*

Step 3: Paraphrase. To clarify your understanding of the speech, using the same two-column format shown in the following example, paraphrase the speech into your own words. This format will help you be sure that your paraphrase covers all the ideas in the speech in the same order they are in the play. (This is important.) None of us is as good a writer as Shakespeare, so our paraphrases can seem insipid compared to his masterly verse. This is not a competition, however. It is a good way to elucidate *for yourself* the implications of lines that may seem obscure or opaque at first. It is how you discover your understanding of the character. Don't be surprised if it takes you more words to say the same thing than it took Shakespeare. Economy is one of his many virtues that we may not be able to imitate. What follows is my own paraphrase of the "To be or not to be" soliloquy. It is *not* definitive! I am rendered humble by realizing how much lesser my version is than Shakespeare's, but it did help me see the speech more clearly for myself. It is included here to give you an

Figure 3. Contained within the speeches of Shakespeare's plays is some of the most vital, thrilling, exhilarating, profound, and hilarious material imaginable for actors. Tom Hulce as Hamlet at The Shakespeare Theatre in Washington, DC. Used by permission of photographer Joan Marcus.

idea of how these exercises look, *not* because my interpretation of this speech will open new critical vistas.

To be, or not to be—that is the question:	To live or to just give up, that is the issue here:
Whether 'tis nobler in the mind to suffer	In the long run, is it better to put up with

The slings and arrows of
outrageous fortune,
Or to take arms against a sea
of troubles,
And by opposing end them?
To die, to sleep—
No more; and by a sleep to
say we end
The heartache and the
thousand natural shocks
That flesh is heir to—'tis a
consummation
Devoutly to be wished: to die,
to sleep.
To sleep, perchance to dream.
Ay, there's the rub;
For in that sleep of death
what dreams may come,
When we have shuffled off
this mortal coil,
Must give us pause. There's
the respect
That makes calamity of so
long life.
For who would bear the whips
and scorns of time,
The oppressor's wrong, the
proud man's contumely,
The pangs of disprized love,
the law's delay,
The insolence of office, and
the spurns
That patient merit of the
unworthy takes,
When he himself might his
quietus make
With a bare bodkin? Who
would these fardels bear,
To grunt and swear under a
weary life,
But that the dread of something
after death,

all the unfairness that life
deals out,
or to fight back against huge
odds
and by killing yourself, stop
the pain? To end it all—
Stop the pain; as easily as
going to sleep to stop
the thing after thing after
thing
that being human forces on
us—that would be
all we could hope for. Just
like dozing off,
drifting off to dreamland. Ah,
but there's the problem.
Not knowing what kind of
dreams
we'd have after we died

stops us. It is that worry that
leads
to the "disaster" of a long life.

Honestly, who would put up
with it—
the power trips and
oppression,
the rejection, the official
corruption,
the dishonesty, and the
contempt dealt us
constantly,

when it could so easily be
ended with one
little knife? Who'd take it?

Who'd put up with it all

if it wasn't for fear of what
happens

The undiscovered country, from whose bourn
No traveler returns, puzzles the will,
And rather makes us bear those ills we have
Than fly to others we know not of?
Thus conscience does make cowards of us all;
And thus the native hue of resolution
Is sickled o'er with the pale cast of thought,
And enterprises of great pith and moment
With this regard their currents turn away
And lose the name of action.— Soft you now,
The fair Ophelia. Nymph, in all thy orisons
Be all my sins remembered.

after we die—fear of the other side,
from which no one returns— the unknown—
that makes us put up with the hell we have
rather than risk something worse?
So in the end we all chicken out.
Our resolution dissolves because of the fears
we dream up about what's out there,
and our great, urgent purpose

stalls and

eventually evaporates. But look.
It's Ophelia. Well, if it isn't Miss
Holier-Than-Thou

Action: Using this same format, paraphrase your speech.

Analysis

Step 4: Make Copies of Your Speech. Using an enlarging photo-copier, make a master copy of your speech in a large print size. (This step can alternately be accomplished by downloading an electronic text of your play from the Internet, cutting and pasting your speech into a separate document and choosing a large type size, double spaced. *Action: Photocopy or print additional copies of the speech, so that you have eight copies.*

Step 5: Consult the Control Text. Using a facsimile edition of the Folio (or of a quarto edition of your text, if that is the control text used by your editor), look at the original published form of your speech and compare it to its current form. *Action: Using a red pen, mark all the original punctuation on the first of your copies. Using a second color, mark other interesting changes from the original edition, which might include such things as wording, spellings, capitalizations, and stage directions. Using a third color, highlight or underline all material added by modern editors, which (you will probably discover) includes most stage directions.*

Step 6: Scansion. If your speech is in verse, scan it into iambic pentameter. *Action: On your second copy, highlight any elisions, expansions, or other variations you discover that require you to take special action as an actor. Using a different color, underline all opening and line end variations. Make special note of any half-lines.* (The following example shows the scansion of the first nine lines of Hamlet's most famous soliloquy. The results are footnoted here, but you will mark them directly on your speech.)

> To be, or not to be—that is the quest(ion):
> 'Whether 'tis nobler in the mind to suf(fer)
> The slings and arrows of outrageous for(tune),
> 'Or to take arms against a sea of troub(les),
> And by opposing end (them)? To die, to sleep–   5
> No more; and by a sleep to say we end
> The heartache and the thousand natural shocks
> That flesh is heir to—'tis a consumma(tion)
> Devoutly to be wished: to die, to sleep.   9

1. Opening variation at mid-line, line end variation 2. Opening variation, ending variation 3. Ending variation 4. Opening variation, ending variation 5. Ending variation at mid-line 7. *Nat'ral* 8. Ending variation

Step 7: Finding the Structure. Look at the speech for its natural beginning, middle, and end structure. Notice the development of the argument in the middle section of the speech. Observe the rise and fall of specific lines of thought. *Action: On the third copy of your speech, divide the speech into actor's "beats." Highlight the thesis or question that occurs in the start of the speech. Also highlight any statement of conclusion.*

Step 8: Important Words. Looking over your speech, decide which is the most important word of each line. In rare cases, you may need to choose two, but work simply. Beware of the trap of choosing personal pronouns. Such pronouns rarely receive the stress in early modern drama. *Action: On copy four, mark the most important word in each line. This is the word you will stress most heavily when you speak the line.*

Step 9: Finding the Antitheses. Look over your speech to find all the antitheses in it. This may take a bit of sleuthing, as the two parts of a comparison or contrast do not always sit side by side. Shakespeare, especially, was fond of splitting them apart and putting a separate clause between them. *Action: Find the first thesis and circle it in colored pen on copy 5. Find the counterpart antithesis and circle it in the same color. Connect the two with a line. Now, using a different color, look for the second antithesis pair and do the same. Using a third color, circle the third pair. Continue in this fashion to the speech's end. The purpose of using so many colors is to try to minimize the confusion that arises when one pair is nested inside another, as they frequently are.*

Step 10: Finding the Other Verbal Devices. Continue finding verbal and literary conceits in the speech. You will be looking especially for patterns of assonance and alliteration. Next, search out rhymes, half-rhymes, internal rhymes, and historic rhymes. Finally look for jokes and puns. *Action: On copy 6 of your speech, use one color to underline assonance and alliteration. Using a separate color, highlight the rhymes. Using a third color, highlight jokes, puns, and wordplay that may be of special interest.*

Step 11: Imagery. Examine the speech for the images used within it. What kinds of metaphors are employed? Do the images cluster together into any identifiable pattern? Are they related to each other? *Action: Using copy 7 of your speech, circle the major images in the piece. Where they are related to other images, connect the clusters with linking lines.*

Step 12: Acting Concerns. As a final step, think through this piece as you might any other bit of acting material to determine your character's objectives. Why are you (as the character) speaking? What do you hope to accomplish? Where are you coming from? What has happened in the plot that sets up this speech? *Action: Using your final copy, write the "moment before" information at the top of the page. In the margins, make a chart of your objectives.*

Research

Step 13: Literary Research. Look at the notes in several different editions for ideas concerning your speech. The Arden and individual Oxford editions are particularly good for this. If you have access to a Variorum in your library, check it. *Action: Write down your top three discoveries from research.*

Step 14: Performance History. Check into the history of performances of this speech. There are a number of series that examine specific plays in performance, and other series in which actors discuss their approaches to particular roles. Find out what you can about what other actors have done with this speech. *Action: Write down your top three discoveries from performance history research.*

An Example Preparation

To illustrate some of the results of such a preparation, the following pages will reflect some of the results that might come from such a preparation of the opening speech of *Henry V*, which is delivered by the character "Chorus."

The speech goes as follows:

Henry V

O for a Muse of fire, that would ascend
The brightest heavens of invention!
A kingdom for a stage, princes to act,
And monarchs to behold the swelling scene!   4
Then should the warlike Harry, like himself,
Assume the port of Mars, and at his heels
(Leashed in like hounds) should famine, sword and fire
Crouch for employment. But pardon, gentles all,   8
The flat unraised spirits that hath dared
On this unworthy scaffold to bring forth
So great an object. Can this cockpit hold
The vasty fields of France? Or may we cram   12
Within this wooden O the very casques
That did affright the air at Agincourt?
O, pardon! Since a crooked figure may
Attest in little place a million,   16

And let us, ciphers to this great accompt,
On your imaginary forces work.
Suppose within the girdle of these walls
Are now confined two mighty monarchies,   20
Whose high, upreared, and abutting fronts
The perilous narrow ocean parts asunder.
Piece out our imperfections with your thoughts;
Into a thousand parts divide one man,   24
and make imaginary puissance;
Think, when we talk of horses, that you see them
Printing their proud hoofs i'th' receiving earth;
For 'tis your thoughts that now must deck our kings,   28
Carry them here or there, jumping over times,
Turning th' accomplishments of many years
Into an hour glass: for the which supply
Admit me Chorus to this history;   32
Who prologue-like, your humble patience pray
Gently to hear, kindly to judge, our play.   34

1. Opening variation 2. *Invention* is expanded to four syllables. 3. Opening variation at mid-line 8. *Employ(ment)* uses the line end variation at mid-line. 9.
Unraisèd is expanded to three syllables. 16. *Million* is expanded to three syllables.
21. *Uprearèd* is expanded to three syllables. 22. *Per'lous* is elided to two syllables,
line-ending variation. 25. Line end variation 26. Opening and ending variations
27. Opening variation; *i'th'* elides to one syllable, rhyming with *with*. 29. Opening variation, *over* contracts to "o'er," rhyming with *for*. 30. Opening variation; *th'*
contracts into *accomplishments*, so the two words take up four syllables. 31. *(Glass)*
is an end variation at mid-line. 32. *History* is an historic rhyme, making a couplet
with the previous line. 34. *Gently* and *kindly* both employ the opening variation.

Step 1: Putting the Speech in Context. This speech is the opening of the play. In it, the character of Chorus comes forward to prepare the audience for what is coming and to ask them to use their
imaginative powers to help with the dramatic enterprise. This character is our friend and guide.

Step 2: Clarifying Meanings. There are many words and phrases
that may be unfamiliar in this piece. A few examples might be *casques*
(helmets) in line 13, *Agincourt* (site of Henry V's most famous military victory) in line 14, and *puissance* (literally, power, but here metaphorically meaning troops) in line 25. Some phrases are composed
of words we know, but their combined meaning can be difficult, for

example *Muse of fire* (poetic invention) from line 1, *port of Mars* (the attitude of the War God) from line 6, and *wooden O* (a reference to the circular theater of Shakespeare's time) from line 13. (Footnotes in the Norton Shakespeare and the OED supplied these definitions.)

Step 3: Paraphrase. In the interest of space, a full, two-column paraphrase is not repeated here, since an example has already been provided. Quickly speaking, however, this speech includes the plea of Chorus to the audience to use their imaginations to help fill out the dramatic spectacle. Chorus tells us that the play and the theater cannot produce events on the scale of the war portrayed in this piece, but imagination can extend the actor's suggestions into a moving spectacle.

Step 4: Make Copies. Not applicable.

Step 5: Consulting the Control Text. Though there were three quartos published prior to the Folio, they are all "bad" quartos without authority. The control text is the Folio. It contains an extensive number of differences from the modern version printed here. The punctuation varies greatly, and though there is no reason to think the Folio contains Shakespeare's authoritative version, the phrasing is rhetorically helpful. There are also many spelling and capitalization differences. There are no stage directions but "Enter Prologue" and "Exit" in the Folio.

Step 6: Scansion. The scansion for this piece appears immediately under the text for easy consultation. Lines 2 and 16 contain expansions that the actor may choose to ignore because they occur at the line's end, where other words do not depend on them, and they create an unusual sound, though I would opt for keeping both. Line 32 contains an historic rhyme, which, because I suspect it would sound comic rather than antique, I would not keep in performance.

Step 7: Finding the Structure. This speech invokes a typical beginning-middle-end structure. It calls on the muse of poetic inspiration in the first line. Much of the speech develops this idea by giving specific examples of historic elements and events that will be portrayed, which will need the imaginative cooperation of the audience to seem complete. The speech ends by specifically asking the audience to be cooperative and kind.

Step 8: Important Words. As examples, I might choose *Muse* in the first line as the most important word. *Invention* would get my nod in the second line. (Notice, already, that these two are related.) *Kingdom, Princes*, and *Monarchs* would be my next choices. (This again is a related cluster.)

Step 9: Finding the Antitheses. As examples, the first eight lines of this speech, which paint a brilliant picture of pageantry, are contrasted in the next eight with the poor means available to portray it. These are larger pieces than usual, but they make interesting antitheses because of their size. Lines 9–10 (unworthy scaffold/great object) and 10–11 (cockpit/vasty fields) do this same thing in smaller, more easily spotted packages.

Step 10: Verbal Devices. There are many sound clusters of interest, for example, *Harry/himself/heels/hounds* in lines 5–6. There is some interesting wordplay having to do specifically with the numbers—*Wooden O, crooked figure, cipher*—which culminates in the word *accompt*, which punningly means "account" in both of its modern senses (an account as a story and account as in "bank account").

Step 11: Imagery. The central imagery of this piece is that of the theater itself. There is much talk of acting, pretending, imagining, and playing.

Step 12: Acting Concerns. Chorus' purpose is to enlist the audience into using their imaginations and to excite their interest. I'd try to charm them a bit, dare them a bit, and play on their sympathies all I could.

Step 13: Literary Research. The literary commentary is extensive, as this is one of the most imaginative speeches in the entire canon. Again, just one example will have to suffice: Stanley Wells points out that we might not need to take the pleas for scant means too seriously.[2] He contends that the effect of this speech is to glorify the subject matter of the play rather than to point out the theater's inadequacy. It is all a clever device to build up Henry!

Step 14: Performance History. Two quick, interesting facts here: The respected scholar Don Foster,[3] whose work with computers has brought to light many formerly uncovered aspects of the plays, contends that this was a role Shakespeare himself played. Its performance history starts with the author himself.

Of great interest to me is that from the mid-1800s to the 1930s or so, this role was regularly performed by women. It is one of the roles in the canon with the longest history of performance by both genders, which is one of the reasons it has been chosen as the example for this chapter.

These two facts may not tell us exactly what to do with the piece, but both are evocative hints of possibilities that may help to open our thinking.

Rehearsing the Piece

The preceding steps prepared you to work. They are the head work—the initial exploration. The next step is to get on to your feet. Like many actors, I find the process of actually rehearsing the most enjoyable part of what I do, and I suspect that you might find this stage thoroughly pleasurable, too.

Start by memorizing the speech, but do so on your feet. Don't sit and commit the piece to rote memory. It won't be available again when you need it. Instead, try walking as you memorize. Head off across the floor with your first line. When you reach a change of thought, change direction. Begin tracing squares and triangles on the floor with your walking. For a while, just get the speech "in your body." After you have been through the speech several times, set your book aside and see what you already know. Notice that when memory breaks down, it is at the points where thought changes. Walk again, and this time as you turn, pay special attention to the unspoken links between the old thought and the new one. Continue in this fashion, strengthening your recall of the links as well as of the lines.

Once you have the piece learned well enough to free yourself from total dependence on the book, go back to your preparation sheets and try to find the physical equivalent of each of the preparatory stages, as follows:

Step 1: Put the Speech in Context. Imagine the circumstances of the piece and what has happened immediately before the speech. Be sure to image this circumstance every time you start the speech, so that you are coming from somewhere.

Step 2: Clarify Meanings. Speak the speech aloud, with particular attention to the difficult words and passages. Without resorting to symbolic, mimelike behavior, see if you can clarify what you mean when you are saying these words.

Step 3: Paraphrase. Read your own paraphrase aloud. Is it clearer or more lively than your reading of the speech? Read the speech aloud again, seeing if you can retain the best of what the paraphrase brings out in you. Notice that although you may well understand and relate to your own paraphrase better, the verbal devices and verse structure of the speech are more communicative.

Step 4: Making Copies. Not applicable.

Step 5: Consult the Control Text. Holding your copy of the sheet on which you marked the Folio punctuation, read the speech again. This time see what you can learn from this rhetorically based phrasing. Read the speech, taking a quick breath at every comma and a full breath on a colon or semicolon; pause only at periods or other forms of full stops. Notice that these are much longer phrases than contemporary plays usually require. You might repeat this step a couple of times until you feel sure that you see how the phrasing is related to meaning.

Step 6: Scansion. Consulting your scansion copy, speak the selection again, double checking the rhythm where you are in doubt. Attend to the pulse of the piece. Feel how riding the rhythm helps you keep the energy of the piece moving forward.

Step 7: Finding the Structure. While speaking the piece, and trying to retain the discoveries from previous steps, speak the text this time with conscious attention to the beginning-middle-end structure. Choose a specific location to represent the beginning. While you stand in this area, you are asking a question or introducing a theme. Physically move to a new area when you are developing your argument in the middle section. Pace or trace the floor triangles of your memorization step while working in this part. Return to the first area when you bring your speech around to its conclusion. Think of yourself as literally tying up loose ends when you return to the starting place.

Step 8: Important Words. Keeping the structure and rhythm of the speech, see if you can pare your stresses back so that you are hitting only one or two target words per line. (Most people incorrectly think target words need extra stress, but their purpose is to help us correct the contemporary problem of too much stress! We emphasize so many words that everything starts seeming equally important. Less is more.)

Step 9: Finding the Antitheses. With your antithesis sheet in front of you, see if you can physicalize some of these oppositions in literal, "on-the-one-hand" fashion. Indicate the first part of the pairing as taking place to your left, perhaps even taking a few steps or gesturing in that direction. When you come to its counterpart, walk or gesture in the opposite direction. See what you learn.

Step 10: Verbal Devices. As an additional layer to all that has gone before, explore the implications of giving particular emphasis to the verbal devices. Crack the jokes, relish the wordplay, stress the alliteration and assonance. Don't just say the words—choose them. Let Chorus be a character that loves the rhetoric. Rhyme on purpose, not because it is written down. See how this reinforces work you have already done!

Step 11: Imagery. You are very close to full performance now. Take time to fully imagine all the images of the piece. Be sure that you see and feel all of them. What do they mean to you? Can you personalize them?

Step 12: Acting Concerns. If you've done your exploration well, enjoying the steps as you went through them and attending to your accumulating discoveries, you are to the point where you can let the head work go and just perform. Don't worry, your discoveries will stay with you. Step 12 is to pursue your objectives as you would in any other acting circumstance. The goal is not to be "correct" or safe, but to accomplish your goal. Win one for the character! If you are a member of a class or have access to a group of friends, present the piece formally.

Step 13: Literary Research. Once you've performed, just do a quick mental check to see if there is anything from your reading that you would like to add to the presentation. If you were to do it again, are there content ideas that you might explore?

Step 14: Performance History. Now that you've performed and you feel committed to your own choices, compare and contrast these with some made during the performance history of the speech. Never just imitate someone else's performance, but see if there are useful ideas about the piece that you might use to further the lines of choice that you are already making. Try the piece again a couple of times. See how it may be improved.

Performance Guidelines

If you are working in a class or group situation with an instructor, you may well have specific guidelines concerning presentation of your monologues. By all means, follow these.

The following suggestions are offered in the absence of such guidelines to give some direction to those working on their own, or to give a self-directed group a collective starting point.

1. Delineate a performance space. If you don't already have access to a defined theater space, create a small clear space to use for your performance. You can give it some of the features of an early modern playhouse by using a sturdy table or desk in the back of your "stage" to create the two-level look of theaters. (Consult the photos and diagrams in Part III to help envision this space.)

2. Since early modern spaces had no curtain, get used to beginning your presentation by striding confidently into the center of the performance space.

3. Introduce yourself and your piece quickly, loudly, and clearly. It is customary to keep this to a minimum. A typical introduction goes, "I'm [your name], and I'll be playing [character] from [play title, act and scene number]." Thus, "Hello. I'm Kurt Daw and I'll be playing Brutus from *Julius Caesar*, Act One, Scene Two."

For the sake of sharing our learning about the plays, I take the rather unusual step of asking my students to verbally set the situation up a bit in my own classroom. This describing the situation is different than explaining what you are about to do, to which I vehemently object.

A typical one- or two-sentence summary tells the observers the basic information about the situation *preceding* the scene. For Juliet's famous "Gallop, apace" speech, this might go as follows: "Juliet has secretly married Romeo and now awaits his return." It is simple and direct, but might well be new information for a class when hearing a selection from a less familiar play. These introductions should never say what is going to happen in the presentation itself, as they can upstage your performance. They are also inappropriate in formal auditions, when your auditors can be assumed to have a familiarity that renders this unnecessary.

4.   Take a breath and begin the presentation. For a soliloquy or an aside, address the audience directly. For a monologue, speak to an imaginary partner placed in front of you.

5.   The conventions of both classrooms and the early modern theater dictate that your use of props and furniture be limited to an absolute minimum. The rule of thumb is to use only what you can carry on with you, produce naturally within the context of the piece, and remove when you are done, such as a handkerchief or a pocket watch. A single chair is usually provided in formal auditions, but I recommend that you *do not* use it.

6.   At the end of your piece, use the single word *curtain* to indicate that you have finished. Say "Thank you" to your observers and stride confidently off.

Frequently Asked Questions for Monologues

Q: How long should my piece be?
A: Of course, the answer to every question should begin with the words *it depends*, but I'll ask you to bear in mind that all of these answers are subject to some variation to meet certain circumstances and give some (perhaps overly) specific advice.
A typical performance speed is seventeen lines in one minute, not including the time the introduction takes. In classrooms and auditions, selections of fourteen to fifty lines

are standard. If there are specific time limits, you can calculate for yourself the longest possible piece. (A two-minute limit, for example, dictates that the piece should be no longer than thirty lines, to leave time for your introduction.) Most beginning Shakespeareans choose pieces that are too long for their first attempts. I suggest fifteen to twenty-five lines the first time out.

Q: Does the piece have to be in verse?
A: Not necessarily, but if it isn't, the listener won't know anything about your ability to handle verse. In auditions in which you hope to be cast to play a character whose lines are largely in verse, or for graduate schools, a prose selection is unhelpful in establishing your abilities. For this reason, the term *classical* in instructions or notices is usually a code that means "blank verse." In the classroom, verse is also usually preferred, but the rule is more flexible. There are many superb early modern pieces in prose that you may want to explore for your own purposes, as long as the whole point of the exercise is not gearing up for verse work.

Q: I can't seem to find a piece that is right for me. Can you recommend a selection?
A: This is the question I hear more frequently than any other. I've never met an actor (even an experienced professional) for whom selecting a monologue was easy. Despite the seeming difficulty, however, there really is a plethora of possibilities out there. Shakespeare alone wrote thirty-eight plays, with a combined total of hundreds of parts from which to choose. When you look into the works of his contemporaries, you get several times that amount again from which to select. The problem is mostly getting to know the plays well enough to be able to sort through this mass of material. The companion volume to this book is designed to make this task easier, by suggesting common selections from a vast range of plays from the early modern period. These are indexed in ways that may help you narrow your search to a manageable number of possibilities.

The key is starting the selection process early. Look over the plays that hold potential for you. Read through many possibilities and try to familiarize yourself with them *before* you are forced to make a quick decision. It is not unreasonable to think that you could, in a month or less, make a list with material from at least one role from every Shakespeare play. It is not a bad idea for you to have thought through your potential casting in the entire canon. You'll find that such a list could save a huge number of hurry-up-and-choose headaches in the future.

If time has already run out, and you have to decide by, say, tomorrow, then my panic-alleviating advice is to narrow your search to the comedies immediately. (This is based on an educated guess that you don't have time to learn all the stuff going on in the histories overnight, and on the conviction that most of the overdone and astonishingly difficult material is from the tragedies.) There is surely a perfect piece for you in the comedies.

Q: That is all well and good to say, but isn't it true that there isn't much material for women?
A: Female characters in Shakespeare are outnumbered by male characters by a ratio of something like 10 to 1, so, yes, it is true that there is less material specifically for women. My recommendation to my own students is that they look carefully to see if favorite passages and interesting possibilities must be spoken in a male persona. For example, I see no real reason why John of Gaunt's beautiful speech about England (*Richard II*, II.i.31–68) can't be spoken by a woman as well as a man, at least in the classroom. For that matter, on those terms, I don't really see an impediment to a woman delivering some of Henry V's famous speeches. (This is not to say that I think the issue of gender is transparent in all speeches. I admit that "Frailty, thy name is woman" is going to be somehow different coming from a woman than from a man. But many speeches are fair game for everyone.) Once this is taken into account, the amount of material available to women opens up immediately. Be open-minded, and select challenging material.

Q: Should I select characters who are like I am?

A: It is standard advice in beginning acting classes to play characters close to you in age, temperament, and personality, so you can learn to play truthfully. As you advance in your study, it is less likely that this guideline will continue to apply as tightly. For one reason, very few characters in early modern drama are going to be that much like you. They are from plays written in a different time and place and are often set in exotic locales.

I generally recommend, however, that you do choose from characters that you are skilled enough to be, at least potentially, castable. Few beginners are going to play King Lear.

There are terrific characters that are often overlooked in classes and training work because they are smaller, but these are often the most rewarding. (If you are only going to play twenty-five lines of a character, it really doesn't matter if you select them from a part that has several hundred or not. You don't get credit for the rest of the role anyway. Some of those little gems, like messengers whose whole part is one terrific speech, can be very rewarding for the purposes of this exercise.

Q: Why don't you recommend using the chair?

A: Primarily because on the flexible stage of Shakespeare's time, furniture was rarely used. Pieces often look strangely "inauthentic" when performed sitting. Also, I find that many students who want to use it are compensating for not knowing what to do with their bodies. Thinking through the physicalization of the piece is a better solution to this problem.

Q: Where do I look?

A: This is a highly debated question, with a lot of possible answers. The simple answer is to look where the piece tells you to. In monologues, place invisible partners in front of you and look at them (therefore forward.) In soliloquies, look directly toward the audience and engage them. The exception to this rule is auditions. It is always inappropriate, in an audition, to perform so directly to your auditors that they are required to perform back to you.

Q: How can I stop my stage fright?
A: You can't, but you also don't want to. Stage fright is just the energy that will become your performance waiting to manifest itself. It is both normal and healthy. Just notice that stage fright usually occurs before, not during, the performance. Once you get "on," the butterflies will settle down. Trying to control or stop it just makes you notice it more. Keep your mind on what you want to accomplish, rather than on how you feel about it, and you'll be fine.

It may be useful to note that many performers who are attempting early modern drama for the first time feel a renewal of stage fright problems that they had grown beyond in their earlier work. The additional challenges of the work raise the stakes a bit, and a degree of self-consciousness can return. It will pass quickly.

Q: Should I move around during my piece?
A: You should live the part, which will invariably mean that you will physicalize it. That may or may not involve movement about the stage when you suit the action to the word. (The common advice to stand still is really just an instruction not to wander randomly about the stage.) Spend some time thinking about situation, character, and intention and it will become clear to you what you are doing during the piece. Doing that will create a compelling physicality without randomness.

Summing Up

Congratulations on working your way through a first monologue. These steps may seem elaborate, and indeed you may find that you tailor this exercise to your own interests and abilities in the future, but for now, you have had the opportunity to work a speech in a thorough way. Your patience and diligence will be rewarded with your having a piece in your repertory that you really know well, as well as a model in hand for complete exploration of a piece. You can use the steps of this exercise, individually or collectively, to look at any future piece of complex text.

Notes

1. This guide is adapted from an original by Audrey Stanley of the University of California–Santa Cruz, and former artistic director of Shakespeare Santa Cruz. Professor Stanley is an extraordinary teacher whose approaches to performing Shakespeare have deeply influenced my thinking throughout this volume, though she is in no way responsible for any heresies I may be spreading.

2. In *Shakespeare: A Life in Drama*, p. 152.

3. On the Shaxicon Web page.

Further Reading

Jackson, Russell, and Robert Smallwood, eds. 1985–1991. *Players of Shakespeare.* (3 volumes). American editions published in New York: Cambridge University Press.

Sher, Antony. 1987. *Year of the King: An Actor's Diary and Sketchbook.* New York: Limelight Editions.

7 Interacting: Working with Intimate Scenes

This chapter concentrates on partner work in Shakespearean scenes that are placed in solitary settings, where two characters can speak to each other without having to please or impress anyone but their partner. These scenes are a logical next step from monologues, having only a slightly larger focus. The setting is "intimate," in the sense that the characters' interaction is direct and personal. This terminology is adopted to distinguish these scenes from the kind we will be looking at in the next chapter, where the characters are placed in highly public situations for their interactions.

Why Scenes?

The study of acting has traditionally encompassed scene study for the very good reason that two-person scenes allow actors to experience most of the challenges of plays without requiring the logistically difficult organization of a full play. A nearly full range of the skills of acting can be heavily explored in scenes.

Solo work, such as that we have done in sonnets and monologues, can prepare the way well and allow for exploration of many

Figure 4. Two person scenes allow actors to experience nearly the full range of challenges of plays. Eric Ladd as Ariel and Jack Mason as Prospero in a Classic TheaterWorks production of The Tempest, *directed by the author. Design by Ming Chen. Photo courtesy of the designer.*

of the challenges of groundwork and characterization. Interaction, however, requires a partner. This is one of the fundamental components of acting. Scene work will allow us to explore the ways in which early modern plays facilitate that interaction above and beyond the normal means we are used to in contemporary work.

Preparatory Work

The initial stages of looking over a text and examining the textual features that aid our acting were thoroughly explored in the last chapter. Such work is recommended again here, preferably completed in tandem with a partner. For reasons that will become clear as this chapter progresses, it is extremely useful to prepare *both* parts in the scene, not just the part you will be playing.

Throughout this chapter we will be using one of the most famous scenes in the canon as our example, the balcony scene (II.i) from *Romeo and Juliet*. It should be said from the outset that much of the work that must be done in rehearsal for any play (such as blocking, discovering the relationships, and the plain old grunt work of repeating the scene until it is committed to memory and well paced) must be done for Shakespearean scenes as well. These steps will be only lightly considered here.[1] This chapter will concentrate more heavily on examining the specifics of *this* scene and exploring its particularly Shakespearean features. The emphasis will be on the manner in which actors can catch relationship and acting clues from the text.

Beginning the Scene: Embedded Stage Directions

This scene begins with twenty-five lines of extended aside from Romeo, which may at first appear not to affect Juliet at all. Let us look a little closer at them, however, to see why the actor playing Juliet may have as much interest in them as does Romeo.

Romeo and Juliet

ROMEO: He jests at scars that never felt a wound.
         [JULIET *appears above at a window*]
         But, soft! what light through yonder window breaks?
         It is the east, and Juliet is the sun.
         Arise, fair sun, and kill the envious moon,
         Who is already sick and pale with grief,   5
         That thou her maid art far more fair than she:
         Be not her maid, since she is envious;
         Her vestal livery is but sick and green
         And none but fools do wear it; cast it off.
         It is my lady, O, it is my love!   10
         O, that she knew she were!
         She speaks yet she says nothing: what of that?
         Her eye discourses; I will answer it.
         I am too bold, 'tis not to me she speaks:
         Two of the fairest stars in all the heaven,   15

> Having some business, do entreat her eyes
> To twinkle in their spheres till they return.
> What if her eyes were there, they in her head?
> The brightness of her cheek would shame those stars,
> As daylight doth a lamp; her eyes in heaven   20
> Would through the airy region stream so bright
> That birds would sing and think it were not night.
> See, how she leans her cheek upon her hand!   23

The scene begins with Romeo already on stage, and his first line is a reference to Mercutio, who is just exiting after having been unable to find Romeo.

Line 2 contains a reference to a new action—light breaking through Juliet's window. Romeo doesn't cause this, he just notices it. Modern editions (as in our example) may well contain a stage direction here telling Juliet to enter, but this has been added by an editor.[1] Shakespeare has placed the implied stage direction *within* the text. This technique is used more often in early modern texts than the modern convention of numerous and extensive stage directions. On the most fundamental level, then, you can see one of the reasons that actors need to prepare the entire scene (not just their own part), because their stage directions are often buried in other actors' lines.

Looking at Romeo's speech, in this case, there seems some room for doubt as to when Juliet makes her appearance. Something must happen at line 2 to catch Romeo's attention, and Juliet must surely be firmly in place at line 10, but within those parameters there is some variability. In a production I directed of this play, Juliet's silhouette appeared on the sheer curtains behind her window (as if thrown there by a candle she had just carried into the room and set down behind her) at line 2, but she took the next eight lines (while Romeo urged her to "Arise!") to prepare herself before she emerged out onto her balcony. She stepped through the door exactly on the word *O* in the middle of line 10 each night.

At line 12, "She speaks, yet she says nothing; what of that?" there is another implied direction for an action that Juliet must cause. Whatever action Juliet takes probably occurs just before the line, as Romeo's previous line is only six syllables long. The missing four syllables may well indicate a pause. (More on this point later.) She is apparently on the verge of speaking aloud, and then stops.

The Scene Continues: Shared Lines

ROMEO: O, that I were a glove upon that hand,
                That I might touch that cheek!
JULIET: Ay me!
ROMEO: She speaks: 25
                O, speak again, bright angel! for thou art
                As glorious to this night, being o'er my head
                As is a winged messenger of heaven
                Unto the white-upturned wondering eyes
                Of mortals that fall back to gaze on him   30
                When he bestrides the lazy-pacing clouds
                And sails upon the bosom of the air.   32

Of particular interest in this section is line 25. Notice that this is all one iambic pentameter line, but it is shared between the two actors. Romeo speaks the first six syllables, Juliet the next two, and Romeo the last two. As a general rule, shared lines are paced without pause, so that each of the actors must pick up their cues. There are occasional reasons to take an internal pause in the line, but it is a good rule of thumb to treat such careful patterning by the author as a hint that he expected these lines to flow smoothly together. The author is more apt to write a partial line for one character, and start fresh with a complete line for the other character when wishing to indicate a pause. Here is a brief extract from *Twelfth Night* that shows how this works:

ORSINO: How dost thou like this tune?
VIOLA: It gives a very echo to the seat
                Where love is throned.
ORSINO: Thou dost speak masterly. (*The previous two half-lines make one full line, so the indication is not to pause yet.*)
                My life upon't, young though thou art, thine eye
                Hath stayed upon some favor that it loves.
                Hath it not, boy?
VIOLA: A little, by your favor.
                (*These two half -lines make one full line, so no pause*)
ORSINO: What kind of woman is't?
VIOLA: Of your complexion.
                (*These two half-lines make one full line, still no pause*)
ORSINO: She is not worth thee, then. What years i'faith?

VIOLA: (*Pause, pause, pause, pause.*) About your years, my lord.
ORSINO: Too old, by heaven. Let still the woman take
          An elder than herself. (*Scene continues*)

In this example, there are three shared lines where the poetic indication is to keep the pace going. Viola's line, "About your years, my
lord," is only six syllables long, however. When Orsino again speaks,
he has a full pentameter line. The indication is that there are four silent beats, a pause, which the actor can take before she speaks or which
can be left just after her line, whichever has the greater dramatic effect.

There is no rule of verse speaking that is so ironclad that it must
be unthinkingly employed in every situation, but for rehearsal purposes, one probably ought to try to pick up the cues on shared lines
and delay the pauses until they are written into short lines. This will
help you see the shape of the verse, even when it is shared between
you and a partner. Performance choices can then develop out of
what emerges.

Returning to *Romeo and Juliet* you'll notice shared lines (and
questions about what is implied by them) arise at several points in
the scene, like line 91, for example, and a number of lines near the
scene's end.

Relationship Clues: Thees, Thous, and the Like

JULIET: O Romeo, Romeo! wherefore art thou Romeo?
          Deny thy father and refuse thy name;
          Or, if thou wilt not, be but sworn my love,
          And I'll no longer be a Capulet.   35
ROMEO: Shall I hear more, or shall I speak at this?
JULIET: 'Tis but thy name that is my enemy;
          Thou art thyself, though not a Montague.
          What's Montague? it is nor hand, nor foot,
          Nor arm, nor face, nor any other part   40
          Belonging to a man. O, be some other name!
          What's in a name? that which we call a rose
          By any other name would smell as sweet;
          So Romeo would, were he not Romeo call'd,
          Retain that dear perfection which he owes   45
          Without that title. Romeo, doff thy name,

And for that name which is no part of thee
Take all myself.

ROMEO: I take thee at thy word:
Call me but love, and I'll be new baptized;   50
Henceforth I never will be Romeo.

JULIET: What man art thou that thus bescreen'd in night
So stumblest on my counsel?

ROMEO: By a name
I know not how to tell thee who I am:
My name, dear saint, is hateful to myself,   55
Because it is an enemy to thee;
Had I it written, I would tear the word.

JULIET: My ears have not yet drunk a hundred words
Of that tongue's utterance, yet I know the sound:
Art thou not Romeo and a Montague?   60

ROMEO: Neither, fair saint, if either thee dislike.

JULIET: How camest thou hither, tell me, and wherefore?
The orchard walls are high and hard to climb,
And the place death, considering who thou art,
If any of my kinsmen find thee here.   65

ROMEO: With love's light wings did I o'er-perch these walls;
For stony limits cannot hold love out,
And what love can do that dares love attempt;
Therefore thy kinsmen are no let to me.

JULIET: If they do see thee, they will murder thee.   70

ROMEO: Alack, there lies more peril in thine eye
Than twenty of their swords: look thou but sweet,
And I am proof against their enmity.

JULIET: I would not for the world they saw thee here.

ROMEO: I have night's cloak to hide me from their sight;   75
And but thou love me, let them find me here:
My life were better ended by their hate,
Than death prorogued, wanting of thy love.   78

In this section of the scene, Juliet first speaks Romeo's name aloud, but without knowing he has leapt the orchard wall and is within earshot. Romeo speaks to her, and she recognizes his voice. At first, her concern is mostly for his safety, knowing he could be killed if he is caught trespassing, but his elegant language calms her.

This scene is full of archaic pronoun forms—thee, thou, thy, thine, thyself—which can be unsettling to the modern actor. Though they may seem strange at first, their presence is an important clue to the characters' relationships. These older forms are not just old-fashioned ways of saying *you* and *your*, but indicate a closer degree of intimacy. Such usage remains in several European languages, but has now passed from the English language. In Shakespeare's time, however, one still used *you* to address someone more formally and *thee* and *thou* to suggest less rigidity.

These clues remain all over Shakespeare's plays and are most helpful. A slightly longer explanation will be necessary before you can use this clue well, however. The rule here is that at every point in which such pronoun forms appear, a character is making a choice whether to use a more or less formal approach. In situations in which a great degree of formality is expected, such as a commoner talking to a king, use of *thee* would not indicate intimacy but disrespect. Likewise a child talking to a parent in such an informal way would indicate a lack of respect.

In our *Romeo and Juliet* scene, we have just the opposite circumstance. These two characters barely know each other, having met only once at a party. It would be appropriate to keep a little social distance and use the formal *you*, but neither of them does so. They are in love, and they speak more intimately than would be expected. One of the things that gives Romeo the courage to speak up from the darkness is having heard Juliet speak to him so acceptingly.

One way to think about this use of pronouns, for those of us not accustomed to using these forms, is to translate them into physical equivalents. *You* would be like a handshake, *thee* like a hug. I may have trouble knowing how to address someone with the proper pronoun, but I have a good idea of who I know well enough and am on intimate enough terms with to hug. If the governor were invited to my campus for a speech, I wouldn't dream of hugging him. To do so would be to presume a friendship that didn't exist. He, because of his superior rank, might choose to hug me, and I'd be flattered (if flabbergasted), but I still wouldn't assume that it would be fine for me to go about hugging public figures in the future.

Naming and nicknaming are also some sort of equivalent. My friends and family all call me Kurt, but in formal situations, I am more apt to hear my full name, Curtis, called out. I used to joke that the only times I ever heard anyone say my full name, Curtis David Daw, was when I was about to receive an award, or when my mother was very, very angry!

Romeo and Juliet, under ordinary rules of behavior, are no better acquainted than the handshaking, full-naming stage. The fact that
they use pronoun forms commensurate with hugs or nicknames indicates that they are leaping ahead in degrees of trust and intimacy.

Speaking Memorably: Choosing the Lines

JULIET:	By whose direction found'st thou out this place?	
ROMEO:	By love, who first did prompt me to inquire;	80
	He lent me counsel and I lent him eyes.	
	I am no pilot; yet, wert thou as far	
	As that vast shore wash'd with the farthest sea,	
	I would adventure for such merchandise.	
JULIET:	Thou know'st the mask of night is on my face,	85
	Else would a maiden blush bepaint my cheek	
	For that which thou hast heard me speak to-night	
	Fain would I dwell on form, fain, fain deny	
	What I have spoke: but farewell compliment!	
	Dost thou love me? I know thou wilt say 'Ay,'	90
	And I will take thy word: yet if thou swear'st,	
	Thou mayst prove false; at lovers' perjuries	
	Then say, Jove laughs. O gentle Romeo,	
	If thou dost love, pronounce it faithfully:	
	Or if thou think'st I am too quickly won,	95
	I'll frown and be perverse and say thee nay,	
	So thou wilt woo; but else, not for the world.	
	In truth, fair Montague, I am too fond,	
	And therefore thou mayst think my 'havior light:	
	But trust me, gentleman, I'll prove more true	100
	Than those that have more cunning to be strange.	
	I should have been more strange, I must confess,	
	But that thou overheard'st, ere I was ware,	
	My true love's passion: therefore pardon me,	
	And not impute this yielding to light love,	105
	Which the dark night hath so discovered.	
ROMEO:	Lady, by yonder blessed moon I swear	
	That tips with silver all these fruit-tree tops—	
JULIET:	O, swear not by the moon, the inconstant moon,	
	That monthly changes in her circled orb,	110
	Lest that thy love prove likewise variable.	

ROMEO: What shall I swear by?

JULIET: Do not swear at all;
Or, if thou wilt, swear by thy gracious self,
Which is the god of my idolatry,
And I'll believe thee.

ROMEO: If my heart's dear love—   115

JULIET: Well, do not swear: although I joy in thee,
I have no joy of this contract to-night:
It is too rash, too unadvised, too sudden;
Too like the lightning, which doth cease to be
Ere one can say 'It lightens.' Sweet, good night!   120
This bud of love, by summer's ripening breath,
May prove a beauteous flower when next we meet.
Good night, good night! as sweet repose and rest
Come to thy heart as that within my breast!   124

This section of the scene helps us focus on one of the primary issues of performing early modern drama, as it is rhetorically elaborate. Juliet begins the beat by asking a simple, naturalistic question, meaning nothing more than "Who told you about this courtyard?"

Romeo answers the question by personifying the emotion of Love as his guide and telling Juliet that he would have "adventured" to the ends of the earth for her. This is anything but a naturalistic answer. In order to play it, it is not enough to say the words. It is not enough, even, to mean them ardently. Romeo has to love speaking like this. The actor cannot just say these things because that is what is written down for him. The lines will come off flat and sterile (like Christian speaking Cyrano's poetry) if he does. Instead, Romeo must *choose* to speak elaborately on purpose. He must consciously to try to impress Juliet with his cleverness and his verbal dexterity. If he underplays, he will come off as an uneducated clodhopper, apologizing for his "big" words, and she will be left cold. If, however, he speaks these words to show how intensely he is trying to impress her, then she will swoon! (At least, the actor must believe she will.) Think, if you will, what it would take to make up words like this on the spot. Imagine you are in Romeo's shoes, without lines set down for you. Could you improvise like this? Don't let the dazzling invention of the words fade into complacent acceptance of convention. Romeo doesn't speak like this because it is Shakespearean, but because he longs to impress Juliet. It is crucial to take this step if you want to bring the language to life.

Then look at how Juliet responds! The emotional honesty and directness with which she replies tells us that the she is indeed impressed with Romeo's elaborate metaphor, but that she is afraid of being swept off her feet. He must be sure, she tells him, that he means it. She tells him in her words, also rhetorically extravagant, that she is prepared to throw her lot completely with his. The content of her speech informs us of this, but so does its form. She answers him with the same skill with which he wooed her.

The small quarrel that ends the scene, over whether or not to swear by the moon, is a paraphrased form of the argument that this text is making. Juliet tells Romeo not to emptily choose the conventional way, but to be sure he consciously means what he says. She tells him to be sure of his symbolism, and to use it. (She also tells him not to use symbolism that is not appropriate.) It is good advice, in love and in acting.

In the end, in this scene where they fully fall in love, the characters come to see and understand a great deal about each other. Each of them loves the other in part for his/her command of language. Who wouldn't be dazzled by such rich, affecting speech? The actors should, as themselves and as their characters, love this quality in their partner. It is the thing that brings the scene to life.

Other Voices

ROMEO:	O, wilt thou leave me so unsatisfied?	125
JULIET:	What satisfaction canst thou have to-night?	
ROMEO:	The exchange of thy love's faithful vow for mine.	
JULIET:	I gave thee mine before thou didst request it:	
	And yet I would it were to give again.	
ROMEO:	Wouldst thou withdraw it? for what purpose, love?	130
JULIET:	But to be frank, and give it thee again.	
	And yet I wish but for the thing I have:	
	My bounty is as boundless as the sea,	
	My love as deep; the more I give to thee,	
	The more I have, for both are infinite.	135
	(Nurse calls within)	
	I hear some noise within; dear love, adieu!	
	Anon, good nurse! Sweet Montague, be true.	
	Stay but a little, I will come again.	
	(Exit, above)	

ROMEO:	O blessed, blessed night! I am afeard.	
	Being in night, all this is but a dream,	140
	Too flattering-sweet to be substantial.	
	(Re-enter JULIET, above)	
JULIET:	Three words, dear Romeo, and good night indeed.	
	If that thy bent of love be honourable,	
	Thy purpose marriage, send me word to-morrow,	
	By one that I'll procure to come to thee,	145
	Where and what time thou wilt perform the rite;	
	And all my fortunes at thy foot I'll lay	
	And follow thee my lord throughout the world.	
NURSE:	(Within) Madam!	
JULIET:	I come, anon.—But if thou mean'st not well,	150
	I do beseech thee—	
NURSE:	(Within) Madam!	
JULIET:	By and by, I come:—	
	To cease thy suit, and leave me to my grief:	
	To-morrow will I send.	
ROMEO:	So thrive my soul—	
JULIET:	A thousand times good night!	155
	(Exit, above)	

This section of the scene is really a three-person, rather than a two-person, scene. Though the nurse doesn't appear on stage, her voice is crucially important here. Sometimes, when the comments of the lesser voices are simple *yes* or *no* responses and the like, they can be cut for a classroom exercise. In this case, the Nurse's few lines have no great content, but her threatened interruption redirects the scene. Juliet cannot change direction without this cue. Many rehearsals could take place without this voice, but the final few rehearsals and any presentations will require that these few lines be added.

Many scenes have these smaller contributors. These are still superb scenes, which shouldn't be abandoned because of these minor voices. Just ask a friend or classmate to fill in at the appropriate time, and perhaps attend a preparatory rehearsal or two.

In addition to this large issue, this section of our example scene contains some lovely subtleties. Notice, for instance, Juliet's line, "Three words, dear Romeo." We, like Romeo I suspect, think that she is going to say "I love you." Instead she launches off into a set of instructions that take ten lines (with interruptions) to complete. The effect is comic, but her point is serious. She, of course, never has to say those three little words. We all understand what she means.

Physicalizing and Variants

ROMEO:	A thousand times the worse, to want thy light.
	Love goes toward love, as schoolboys from their books,
	But love from love, toward school with heavy looks.
	(Retiring. Re-enter JULIET, above)
JULIET:	Hist! Romeo, hist! O, for a falconer's voice,
	To lure this tassel-gentle back again! 160
	Bondage is hoarse, and may not speak aloud;
	Else would I tear the cave where Echo lies,
	And make her airy tongue more hoarse than mine,
	With repetition of my Romeo's name.
ROMEO:	It is my soul that calls upon my name: 165
	How silver-sweet sound lovers' tongues by night,
	Like softest music to attending ears!
JULIET:	Romeo!
ROMEO:	My dear?
JULIET:	At what o'clock to-morrow
	Shall I send to thee?
ROMEO:	At the hour of nine.
JULIET:	I will not fail: 'tis twenty years till then. 170
	I have forgot why I did call thee back.
ROMEO:	Let me stand here till thou remember it.
JULIET:	I shall forget, to have thee still stand there,
	Remembering how I love thy company.
ROMEO:	And I'll still stay, to have thee still forget, 175
	Forgetting any other home but this.
JULIET:	'Tis almost morning; I would have thee gone:
	And yet no further than a wanton's bird;
	Who lets it hop a little from her hand,
	Like a poor prisoner in his twisted gyves, 180
	And with a silk thread plucks it back again,
	So loving-jealous of his liberty.
ROMEO:	I would I were thy bird.
JULIET:	Sweet, so would I:
	Yet I should kill thee with much cherishing.
	Good night, good night!

| ROMEO: | Parting is such sweet sorrow, 185 |

ROMEO: Parting is such sweet sorrow, 185
That I shall say good night till it be morrow.
(Exit above)
ROMEO: Sleep dwell upon thine eyes, peace in thy breast!
Would I were sleep and peace, so sweet to rest!
Hence will I to my ghostly father's cell,
His help to crave, and my dear hap to tell.   190
(Exit)

Of course, this entire scene would need to be physicalized on the stage, but this section of the scene gives us a particular problem that helps focus our attention on this matter. At line 159, Juliet re-enters the stage and speaks six lines, which Romeo does not hear. The scene happens at night, so whatever convention is being employed (whether modern or Elizabethan), there is the explanation of darkness for why she does not *see* him. This, however, does not explain why he does not *hear* her. Something in the physical choices about the scene must account for this.

In my production, Romeo believed that Juliet had already left for the last time, and he was already climbing the orchard wall to leave again. He was quite far away from her, and we interpreted that as the reason for his inability to hear. I've recently seen a very good production in which Romeo (fearing discovery) had pulled back into the shadows under the balcony, where he couldn't be seen by Juliet. It was also plausible that he couldn't hear her because he was now directly under her and not where her outwardly directed sound could travel.

It is not, therefore, that there is a "right" decision about how to stage this section. There are many ways to make sense of the scene that fit within its parameters. Some choice must be made, however, to account for Juliet's aside. Finding physical solutions can be as intriguing and exciting as finding the verbal ones in a Shakespearean scene. This is an issue we will revisit in our next chapter.

The final issue we will take up with this example scene, though there are many more we could focus on, is an especially rich set of variants. This play is known to us in both a good quarto, the usual control text, and a reasonably strong (but different) Folio text. The end of the scene is usually printed in the quarto version, but the Folio version makes equal sense in many ways. Here, for example, are lines 183–188 as the speakers are assigned in the Folio:

> ROMEO: I would I were thy bird.
> JULIET: Sweet so would I,
> Yet I should kill thee with much cherishing:
> Good night, good night.
> ROMEO: Parting is such sweet sorrow,
> That I shall say goodnight, till it be morrow.
> JULIET: Sleepe dwell upon thine eyes, peace in thy breast.
> ROMEO: Would I were sleep and peace, so sweet to rest.

You'll notice that the lines are identical but that who says them changes from the usual text. I found this arrangement compelling enough to use it in my own production, in part because I found the splitting of the last couplet more dramatic than the usual arrangement, which gives Romeo both lines. I also found the flow of lines quicker because all changes of subject changed speakers. Usually Juliet is forced to take a huge pause in the middle of her line 185, when it is all assigned to her, in order to change directions.

Looking at variants can be interesting, even when they are not as dramatic as this set is. It is possible your director and your partners may not be as keen as you to change anything, but it is useful to think through the options. It makes you more aware of the possibilities, and even if you settle on the most traditional reading, you are apt to do it with new insight once you have seen the alternative(s).

Performance Guidelines

This example scene has given you an opportunity to look at a range of issues that arise in performance with a partner. From them we can construct a short checklist that will serve as a guide to preparing a scene with a partner. In addition to what you know about preparing scenes from your earlier theatrical experience, these guidelines will help you make the special adjustments needed in early modern drama.

Step 1: With your partner, prepare the text using the steps of the monologue preparation exercise. This is a good way to get used to working cooperatively with a partner, as well as understanding the scene better.

Step 2: Examine the scene carefully for embedded stage directions. Be sure you understand all the actions required by the scene.

Step 3: Look for character and relationship clues, especially in the use of personal pronouns. Explore the characters' relationship and intentions in rehearsal.

Step 4: Look at the verbal devices and think about how you could choose them as a character. For example, instead of reading the rhymes as givens in the text, think about why your character might choose to make a clever rhyme at that point in the scene.

Step 5: Physicalize the scene. You may want to pay special attention to the implications of the Shakespearean stage in Part III of this book. Imagine your scene performed on such a stage. Look at the photographs on pages 120 and 136 to help you visualize the arrangement. Use props and furniture sparingly, as you did in your monologue.

Step 6: Look at the control texts and other early editions for variants. Discuss these with your partner and decide if you want to introduce any of these into your performance choices. If you like any of the possibilities, try them in rehearsal. Before performance, be sure you stabilize what text you will be using and the exact arrangement of lines.

Step 7: Near the end of your rehearsal process, be sure to make arrangements for any additional voices needed to complete your scene.

Step 8: Most of the guidelines from monologues still apply to the actual performance: Use the instructor's specific format if it exists. Begin your presentation by striding confidently into the center of the performance space. Introduce yourself, your partner, and your piece quickly, loudly, and clearly. Typically, the partner who speaks second does the introduction, which goes, "I'm [your name], and my partner is [partner's name]. We'll be performing [play title, act, and scene number]."

At the end of your piece, use the single word *curtain* to indicate that you have finished. Say "Thank you" to your observers and stride confidently off.

Frequently Asked Questions for Intimate Scenes

Q: How long should our piece be?
A: In classrooms, selections seventy-five to 150 lines (five to nine minutes) are standard. If there are different time limits usually observed in your situation, you can calculate for yourself the appropriate length by using the average of seventeen lines per minute.

Q: Does the piece have to be in verse?
A: Scenes are far more apt than monologues to *mix* verse and prose. For a first classroom experience, I recommend a piece that has substantial verse passages, but it does not need to be all in verse.

Q: Can you recommend a particularly good selection?
A: Scenes, like monologues, take time and care to choose. There is superb material available for all categories, though I will admit that it is hard to find many good scenes for two female characters in verse. This is again time to be especially open-minded about whether the male persona is a requirement for the character. Look at Shakespeare's contemporaries, as well as his canon, and plan ahead as far as possible. Be sure that the final choice features you and your partner equally, and that you both feel good about the selection.

Q: Where do I look?
A: In truth, almost no one asks this question about scenes, but they should, because the answer is not always to look at each other. The audience will constantly see you in profile if you do. I recommend that you look through your scene carefully to identify potential moments of direct address to the audience, and if you find some, play them strongly. If, at other moments in the scene, you can find a reason to look forward, thus sharing your face with the audience, do so.

Q: My partner and I don't agree on interpretation. What should we do?
A: There are many possible points for disagreement with

partners. It is not uncommon to have difficulty, for example, finding rehearsal times. Learning to work collaboratively with others in complicated circumstances is a particularly valuable theatrical skill.

In the absence of a director, interpretive differences are the most frequent source of conflict. The theatrical rule is that you never direct a partner, and politely decline to be directed by one. The interpretation of the scene should arise from your shared experience of *playing* the scene. Rehearse your actions in such a way as to influence your partner's performance, and watch and listen carefully to his choices so that you may be fully responsive to them. Even if your partner is playing his character in a way wildly different than you expected, respond to what you get, not what you think you should get. If the choices are so off-the-wall that they seem to make no sense, indulging them will usually make this clear faster than challenging them.

Q: We don't seem to be able to find a good scene that isn't quite a bit longer than you suggest. Should we just do the first part of it?
A: It is a more common choice for the classroom to cut scenes internally to preserve a beginning, a middle, and an end. Be careful to retain the scansion as you cut. Look for repetitious information, minor characters, or exposition setting up later parts of the play as material that may be judiciously trimmed for the training exercise.

Q: Can we update a few words and phrases to make the scene easier to understand?
A: No.

Q: Isn't that a bit harsh?
A: Well, yes, it is a bit blunt. In performance, it is not uncommon for a director or dramaturg to do some subtle editing. While in training, however, it seems to me better to struggle with making the original words and ideas clear than to "fix" them. In the long run, your efforts will serve you better.

Summary

Interaction with a partner has been the focus of this chapter. The basic lesson has been about learning to work cooperatively on a textual level, while your characters are often working competitively on the plot level. Our next chapter will take us even deeper in this direction by looking at a special kind of scene that has strong implications in early modern drama.

Note

1. This is not to imply that the editor is doing anything deceitful. The direction is placed in square brackets [thusly] to indicate that it is a latter addition. The notes at the bottom of the page or the end of the play will probably tell you who inserted the direction, and even when historically it was first proposed. All of that is intended to help, but it is not how Shakespeare accomplished the same task.

8 The World Stage: Public Scenes

Queen Elizabeth once declared in a public speech, "We princes . . . are set on stages in sight and view of all the world duly observed; the eyes of many behold our actions; a spot is soon spied in our garments; a blemish quickly noted in our doings." This passage has far-reaching implications in a number of social arenas, but we can take it at face value that the Queen was very aware of the highly public nature of her life and the lives of her nobles.

As playwrights, Shakespeare and his contemporaries were fascinated with such high-profile, public lives. Their plays sometimes focus on the lives of ordinary individuals in domestic settings, but just as often they look at highly placed men and women whose actions affect not just themselves, but also kingdoms and history. In addition to the kinds of intimate scenes we have been looking at, early modern drama is stocked full of scenes in which characters must face their adversaries in highly public confrontations. The stakes can be quite high because the crowd of bystanders is often fickle and volatile.

For contemporary actors used to working in small-cast, single-set plays, these scenes are both a challenge and a revelation. When the closest we have been to this kind of drama is the occasional trial

Figure 5. Shakespeare plays often involve huge numbers of characters and elaborate pageantry. The Shanghai Drama Institute's production of Titus Andronicus. *Design by Ming Chen, for which she won The Prague International Design Competition. Photo courtesy of the designer.*

scene, confrontations in which kingships are hanging in sway are of a new magnitude altogether.

Many of these scenes involve huge numbers of characters and elaborate pageantry. Look at the first scene of *Richard II*, for example. Here, the entire court is assembled to witness a dispute. In performance, there are often as many as thirty actors on stage to begin this play. The size of the scene is quite large, so it comes as a surprise to realize that it actually involves only four speakers.

As we look closer, it is fascinating to realize that in many such scenes, the number of speakers can be quite limited. It is not unusual, in fact, except for a line or two from a functionary, for such scenes to have only two adversaries speaking. The crowd is present not because we need to hear from them individually, but because their collective reaction is the whole point of the scene. The principals are fighting to sway public opinion, with their fortunes, their offices, and sometimes their lives on the line.

This is great dramatic material, and extracts from it can make for wonderful acting exercises. A number of possible scenes, in which the public confrontation is between two main characters, are suggested in

Kurt Daw and Julia Matthew's *A Guide to Scenes and Monologues from Shakespeare and His Contemporaries* (Portsmouth: Heinemann, 1998). Most need some minor editing or the odd line thrown in by a bystander, but they can be prepared and rehearsed by the two main characters on their own. Later, in classroom or performance exercises, the entire group can chip in to create a full scene. To explain how this might happen, let's look at an example scene from *Richard III*, which will be annotated throughout to help explore the public dynamic of the scene.

In preparation, the actors playing Richard and Anne should meet and rehearse this scene just as they might an intimate scene. It needs textual preparation and rehearsal to settle on general blocking. When the group meets for performance exploration, everyone in the group goes to the stage, initially all as bystanders but Anne and Richard. The scene then is set with two principals and a large on-stage group, whose role is simply defined, in this case as ordinary citizens of the realm.

Richard III

[Enter the corpse of KING HENRY VI, Gentlemen
with halberds to guard it; LADY ANNE being the mourner]

Learning to Be a Crowd

Before the scene even begins, we can see from Folio stage directions that Anne is entering at the head of the funeral procession of the recently assassinated king, her father-in-law, and that the casket is accompanied by a guard. For the purposes of this exercise, choose four of the bystanders at random to become the members of the guard that accompanies her. All the rest of the crowd can go about their "everyday" business.

LADY ANNE:	Set down, set down your honourable load,
	If honour may be shrouded in a hearse,
	Whilst I awhile obsequiously lament
	Th'untimely fall of virtuous Lancaster.
	Poor key-cold figure of a holy king! 5
	Pale ashes of the house of Lancaster!
	Thou bloodless remnant of that royal blood!

Be it lawful that I invoke thy ghost,
To hear the lamentations of Poor Anne,
Wife to thy Edward, to thy slaughter'd son,　　　10
Stabb'd by the selfsame hand that made these
　　wounds!
Lo, in these windows that let forth thy life,
I pour the helpless balm of my poor eyes.
O Cursèd be the hand that made these holes!
Cursèd be the heart that had the heart to do it!　15
Cursèd the blood that let this blood from hence!
More direful hap betide that hated wretch,
That makes us wretched by the death of thee,
Than I can wish to adders, spiders, toads,
Or any creeping venom'd thing that lives!　　　20
If ever he have child, abortive be it,
Prodigious, and untimely brought to light,
Whose ugly and unnatural aspect
May fright the hopeful mother at the view;
And that be heir to his unhappiness!　　　　　25
If ever he have wife, let her he made
A miserable by the death of him
As I am made by my poor lord and thee!
Come, now towards Chertsey with your holy
　　load,
Taken from Paul's to be interrèd there;　　　30
And still, as you are weary of the weight,
Rest you, whiles I lament King Henry's corpse.

Anne's first speech is a remarkably dramatic one, and one that
sounds very unlike what she claims it to be—a spontaneous out-
pouring of grief of a recent widow now struck by tragedy a second
time. Phrases like "obsequiously lament" in line 3, and "be it lawful" in line 8 don't sound much like sudden grieving, but instead
seem to be carefully premeditated phrases. The curses of lines 14–
27, even if they don't identify the murderer, are clearly aimed at establishing an attitude toward the killer. This is not the kind of thing
one says to oneself. After all, Anne already knows all of this. While
performing this section, see what happens if Anne isn't just stopping
randomly on her way to the funeral, but has chosen this place specifically to make a highly public display of her outrage.
　Anne should play this speech to change the behavior of the

crowd. Experiment in rehearsal with shaking them out of their work-a-day routines. The scene specifically plays to the previously uninvolved bystanders. Crowd members can respond honestly. They can go on with their work until she makes the case well enough to attract their attention.

Assigning Stray Lines and Swaying the Crowd

[Enter RICHARD]

RICHARD:	Stay, you that bear the corpse, and set it down.
LADY ANNE:	What black magician conjures up this fiend,
	To stop devoted charitable deeds? 35
RICHARD:	Villains, set down the corpse; or, by Saint Paul,
	I'll make a corpse of him that disobeys.
GENTLEMEN:	My lord, stand back, and let the coffin pass.
RICHARD:	Unmanner'd dog! stand thou, when I command:
	Advance thy halbert higher than my breast, 40
	Or, by Saint Paul, I'll strike thee to my foot,
	And spurn upon thee, beggar, for thy boldness.
LADY ANNE:	What, do you tremble? are you all afraid?
	Alas, I blame you not; for you are mortal,
	And mortal eyes cannot endure the devil. 45
	Avaunt, thou dreadful minister of hell!
	Thou hadst but power over his mortal body,
	His soul thou canst not have; therefore be gone.

In this small section of the scene, we can see specifically the fight for control of the bystanders. Here Richard (who is, of course, the killer, just being cursed so roundly) has entered the scene. He immediately begins ordering the guard about. They are somewhat confused as to how to react. There is one line here, 38, that must be picked up by one of the guard. Since it is only ten syllables, this can be learned and performed on the spot. Anne disputes Richard's control by not only confronting him, but also literally accusing him of the very serious matter of being the devil. She is not speaking metaphorically. In an age in which people believed the devil could appear in human form, she is trying to paint her enemy as evil incarnate. Richard is speaking forcefully to cower the crowd, but Anne is not afraid. She speaks cleverly, playing on the fears of the soldiers and their repulsion for Richard's deformity, to win them over. Notice that Richard and Anne are not yet speaking to each other. They are struggling for control of the members of the guard.

In the exploration of the scene, they should both try to sway the sympathies of the crowd, especially the members of the guard. This section sets up all that follows. Both actors should make a genuine effort to affect their fellow group members. It does not matter if the bystanders do not know the scene, they should simply follow their instincts. Go for the person making the best case.

Choosing Sides

RICHARD: Sweet saint, for charity, be not so cursed.
LADY ANNE: Foul devil, for God's sake, hence, and trouble
        us not;   50
        For thou hast made the happy earth thy hell,
        Fill'd it with cursing cries and deep exclaims.
        If thou delight to view thy heinous deeds,
        Behold this pattern of thy butcheries.
        O, gentlemen, see, see! dead Henry's wounds   55
        Open their congeal'd mouths and bleed afresh!

Richard, here, speaks to Anne, but she stays with her tactic of trying to turn the crowd against him. She sets him up by trying to shame him by exposing the King's body with its stab wounds. The topper, however, is when she calls on a common superstition of the time that even old wounds would bleed freshly in the proximity the killer, an unnatural occurrence caused by the presence of unnatural evil. She "sees" that the wounds are again bleeding and calls it to the attention of the crowd. (Whether they are, or are not, is not verifiable by the audience.) Imagine the power this might have on a crowd of superstitious folks. Richard is suddenly in a very dangerous position.

In classrooms and even occasionally on stage, I've seen this scene played as a private confrontation between two actors. There are, of course, many ways to play a scene, but I've always thought this section of the text makes less sense when played that way. If Anne is exaggerating, it has no effect if there is no crowd to hear her, and if she is telling the truth, and Richard is evil incarnate, why would he care that such a sign exposed him privately? Anne already thinks he is the devil, and he would already know it. Either way, the section works better when it is aimed at listeners.

For exploration purposes, let the crowd overplay their reactions. Crowd members should pick sides and actively root for their choice. The crowd is a third character in this scene. It is their involvement that makes the scene interesting to a real audience and playable for the principals.

The Dynamics of Change

LADY ANNE:	Blush, Blush, thou lump of foul deformity;
	For 'tis thy presence that exhales this blood
	From cold and empty veins, where no blood dwells;
	Thy deed, inhuman and unnatural, 60
	Provokes this deluge most unnatural.
	O God, which this blood madest, revenge his death!
	O earth, which this blood drink'st revenge his death!
	Either heaven with lightning strike the murderer dead,
	Or earth, gape open wide and eat him quick, 65
	As thou dost swallow up this good king's blood
	Which his hell-govern'd arm hath butcherèd!
RICHARD:	Lady, you know no rules of charity,
	Which renders good for bad, blessings for curses.
LADY ANNE:	Villain, thou know'st no law of God nor man: 70
	No beast so fierce but knows some touch of pity.
RICHARD:	But I know none, and therefore am no beast.
LADY ANNE:	O wonderful, when devils tell the truth!
RICHARD:	More wonderful, when angels are so angry.
	Vouchsafe, divine perfection of a woman, 75
	Of these supposèd crimes, to give me leave,
	By circumstance, but to acquit myself.
LADY ANNE:	Vouchsafe, defused infection of a man,
	For these known evils, but to give me leave,
	By circumstance, t'accuse thy cursèd self. 80

Anne builds the public pressure. She is still orating to the crowd. Richard is doing all he can to calm her. He has given up hope that he can win over the crowd. He is now seeking to calm her and contain the damage.

If Richard is successful in calming Anne, those who had responded to her earlier outrage may begin to feel a little abandoned. This is the dynamic of the scene, not a mistake. They were all into her cause, and now it seems to be slipping away from her and them.

Winning Publicly, Losing Privately

RICHARD:	Fairer than tongue can name thee, let me have
	Some patient leisure to excuse myself.
LADY ANNE:	Fouler than heart can think thee, thou canst make
	No excuse current, but to hang thyself.
RICHARD:	By such despair, I should accuse myself. 85
LADY ANNE:	And, by despairing, shouldst thou stand excused;
	For doing worthy vengeance on thyself,
	Which didst unworthy slaughter upon others.
RICHARD:	Say that I slew them not?
LADY ANNE:	Then say they were not slain.
	But dead they are, and devilish slave, by thee. 90
RICHARD:	I did not kill your husband.
LADY ANNE:	Why, then he is alive.
RICHARD:	Nay, he is dead; and slain by Edward's hand.
LADY ANNE:	In thy foul throat thou liest: Queen Margaret saw
	Thy murderous falchion smoking in his blood;
	The which thou once didst bend against her
	breast, 95
	But that thy brothers beat aside the point.
RICHARD:	I was provokèd by her sland'rous tongue,
	which laid their guilt upon my guiltless shoulders.
LADY ANNE:	Thou wast provokèd by thy bloody mind.
	Which never dream'st on aught but butcheries: 100
	Didst thou not kill this king?
RICHARD:	I grant ye.
LADY ANNE:	Dost grant me, hedgehog? then, God grant me too
	Thou mayst be damnèd for that wicked deed!
	O, he was gentle, mild, and virtuous!
RICHARD:	The better for the King of heaven, that hath
	him. 105

There are a great many things going on in this section of the scene. There is brilliant wordplay, wonderful inversions of ideas. Anne is successfully calling Richard's bluff, exposing his lies, and getting him to publicly confess to multiple murder. What is not so often noticed in playing this scene is that Richard is successfully getting Anne to focus on him rather than the crowd. He is pulling her in. She is no longer calling him a devil. He now has the initiative. He is still in danger, but now has some chance to escape it.

Big Choices

LADY ANNE:	He is in heaven, where thou shalt never come.
RICHARD:	Let him thank me, that holp to send him thither;
	For he was fitter for that place than earth.
LADY ANNE:	And thou unfit for any place but hell.
RICHARD:	Yes, one place else, if you will hear me name it. 110
LADY ANNE:	Some dungeon.
RICHARD:	Your bed-chamber.

This is, of course, the most shocking moment of the scene. Richard has the audacity to proposition the young widow of a man he has murdered, and at a funeral of a second relative of hers that he has murdered. It is an outrage. It is also one of the few actions that has any chance of weighing in with the intensity equal to her anger. Richards often play this moment as if they have decided well in advance to come here just for the fun of seeing if they can ruin a good funeral by playing on Anne's weakness, but I suggest the scene is dramatically much more interesting if he is driven to this sudden strategy because it is the best way he can think of to get out of an incredibly dangerous situation. The scene is far more apt to play out this way if the bystanders take an active part in the scene. When they stand like pieces of scenery in the background, Richard and Anne will make up something to give the scene an edge, but if the crowd's opinion is at stake, the scene instantly has this dynamic. Knowing that Shakespeare can write intimate scenes when he chooses, it is better to examine the role of the crowd whenever one is written into a scene.

Going to the Crowd Through the Partner

LADY ANNE:	I'll rest betide the chamber where thou liest!
RICHARD:	So will it, madam till I lie with you.
LADY ANNE:	I hope so.
RICHARD:	I know so. But, gentle Lady Anne,
	To leave this keen encounter of our wits, 115

<blockquote>

	And fall somewhat into a slower method,
	Is not the causer of the timeless deaths
	Of these Plantagenets, Henry and Edward,
	As blameful as the executioner?
LADY ANNE:	Thou art the cause, and most accursed effect. 120
RICHARD:	Your beauty was the cause of that effect;
	Your beauty: which did haunt me in my sleep
	To undertake the death of all the world,
	So I might live one hour in your sweet bosom.
LADY ANNE:	If I thought that, I tell thee, homicide, 125
	These nails should rend that beauty from my cheeks.
RICHARD:	These eyes could never endure sweet beauty's wreck;
	You should not blemish it, if I stood by:
	As all the world is cheerèd by the sun,
	So I by that; it is my day, my life. 130
LADY ANNE:	Black night o'ershade thy day, and death thy life!
RICHARD:	Curse not thyself, fair creature thou art both.

</blockquote>

Wow! Richard tells Anne that she drove him to murder, because he was so totally infatuated with her. We can now see clearly the pattern of the scene. Anne wins if she can stay focused on inciting the crowd to mob action against Richard. Richard wins if he can successfully distract her from her larger purpose and keep her focused on what he says. In this sense, the more outlandish his tactics, the greater his chances that her anger will be so directed at him that she forgets to include the crowd. He, notice now, is subtly beginning to play to the crowd with his extravagant praise of her beauty.

Symbolic Actions

<blockquote>

LADY ANNE:	I would I were, to be revenged on thee.
RICHARD:	It is a quarrel most unnatural,
	To be revenged on him that loveth you. 135
LADY ANNE:	It is a quarrel just and reasonable,
	To be revenged on him that slew my husband.
RICHARD:	He that bereft thee, lady, of thy husband,
	Did it to help thee to a better husband.
LADY ANNE:	His better doth not breathe upon the earth. 140

</blockquote>

RICHARD: He lives that loves thee better than he could.
LADY ANNE: Name him.
RICHARD: Plantagenet.
LADY ANNE: Why, that was he.
RICHARD: The selfsame name, but one of better nature.
LADY ANNE: Where is he?
RICHARD: Here.
             [She spits at him.]

Again, there are many aspects of this section of the scene that would need rehearsal attention. The point is not that all that matters is the public interchange, but focusing on that aspect now, notice that Anne becomes temporarily confused by Richard's fast talk here. He plays on the fact that he was closely related to her husband and has the same last name. When she suddenly realizes what he is proposing, she is no longer confused, however. She spits on the very idea of being married to this monster. Her action is a symbolic statement of her position. All the layers of work we explored in the last chapter occur in this scene, but in addition, it has this new public element.

Symbolic Actions, Continued

RICHARD: Why dost thou spit at me?
LADY ANNE: Would it were mortal poison, for thy sake!   145
RICHARD: Never came poison from so sweet a place.
LADY ANNE: Never hung poison on a fouler toad.
             Out of my sight! thou dost infect my eyes.
RICHARD: Thine eyes, sweet lady, have infected mine.
LADY ANNE: Would they were basilisks, to strike thee dead! 150
RICHARD: I would they were, that I might die at once;
             For now they kill me with a living death.
             Those eyes of thine from mine have drawn salt tears,
             Shamed their aspect with store of childish drops:
             These eyes that never shed remorseful tear,   155
             No, when my father York and Edward wept,
             To hear the piteous moan that Rutland made
             When black-faced Clifford shook his sword at him;
             Nor when thy warlike father, like a child,
             Told the sad story of my father's death,   160
             And twenty times made pause to sob and weep,

That all the standers-by had wet their cheeks
Like trees bedash'd with rain: in that sad time
My manly eyes did scorn an humble tear;
And what these sorrows could not thence
    exhale, 165
Thy beauty hath, and made them blind with
    weeping.
I never sued to friend nor enemy;
My tongue could never learn sweet smoothing
    word;
But now thy beauty is proposed my fee,
My proud heart sues, and prompts my tongue to
    speak. 170
[She looks scornfully at him.]
Teach not thy lips such scorn, for they were made
For kissing, lady, not for such contempt.
If thy revengeful heart cannot forgive,
Lo, here I lend thee this sharp-pointed sword;
Which if thou please to hide in this true
    bosom. 175
And let the soul forth that adoreth thee,
I lay it naked to the deadly stroke,
And humbly beg the death upon my knee.
[He lays his breast open: she offers at [it] with his sword.]
Nay, do not pause; for I did kill King Henry,
But 'twas thy beauty that provokèd me. 180
Nay, now dispatch; 'twas I that stabb'd young
    Edward,
But 'twas thy heavenly face that set me on.
[She lets fall the sword.]
Take up the sword again, or take up me.

The roles have now almost exactly reversed. Richard has brilliantly stolen the scene out from under Anne. He tells a long grief-filled story of the death of his father and his "heartbreaks." He makes a public spectacle of himself, and then makes an explicitly public gesture by baring his breast for her sword. This would make less sense in a private confrontation. It is the public symbolism of what he is doing that makes it important. Anne is now in the position where she must either kill him or be seen by the crowd as accepting him.

Public Positions

LADY ANNE:	Arise, dissembler: though I wish thy death,
	I will not be the executioner. 185
RICHARD:	Then bid me kill myself, and I will do it.
LADY ANNE:	I have already.
RICHARD:	That was in thy rage:
	Speak it again, and, even with the word,
	That hand, which, for thy love, did kill thy
	love, 190
	Shall, for thy love, kill a far truer love;
	To both their deaths thou shalt be accessary.
LADY ANNE:	I would I knew thy heart.
RICHARD:	'Tis figured in my tongue.
LADY ANNE:	I fear me both are false. 195
RICHARD:	Then never man was true.
LADY ANNE:	Well, well, put up your sword.
RICHARD:	Say, then, my peace is made.
LADY ANNE:	That shall you know hereafter.
RICHARD:	But shall I live in hope? 200
LADY ANNE:	All men, I hope, live so.
RICHARD:	Vouchsafe to wear this ring.
LADY ANNE:	To take is not to give.
RICHARD:	Look, how this ring encompasseth finger.
	Even so thy breast encloseth my poor heart; 205
	Wear both of them, for both of them are thine.
	And if thy poor devoted suppliant may
	But beg one favour at thy gracious hand,
	Thou dost confirm his happiness for ever.
LADY ANNE:	What is it? 210
RICHARD:	That it would please thee leave these sad designs
	To him that hath more cause to be a mourner,
	And presently repair to Crosby Place;
	Where, after I have solemnly interr'd
	At Chertsey monastery this noble king, 215
	And wet his grave with my repentant tears,
	I will with all expedient duty see you:
	For divers unknown reasons. I beseech you,
	Grant me this boon.
LADY ANNE:	With all my heart; and much it joys me too, 220
	To see you are become so penitent.
	Tressel and Berkeley, go along with me.
RICHARD:	Bid me farewell.

LADY ANNE:	'Tis more than you deserve;
	But since you teach me how to flatter you,
	Imagine I have said farewell already. 225

[Exeunt LADY ANNE, with TRESSEL and BERKELEY]

The scene ends with Anne softening to her enemy. She is taken in by his act. It is not enough that she not kill him, but Richard makes it explicit that not killing him is tantamount to accepting his suit. This again is not won directly from Anne, but publicly stated so that it becomes an official understanding. She does not so much accept him as just get out of the situation gracefully by moving the funeral along. If Richard had accomplished nothing else, this would have been remarkable enough. He successfully turned around a dangerous situation. It will end with his marriage to Anne, because in addition to distracting her from her purpose, he successfully made the public terms of the scene to either kill him or love him. No middle ground. She doesn't directly agree to this formula, but because she cannot bring herself to kill him, the effect is that she (like the crowd) has come to believe, on some level, that she must love him.

Giving the Scene a Finish

RICHARD:	Sirs, take up the corpse.
GENTLEMEN:	Towards Chertsey, noble lord?
RICHARD:	No, to White-Friars; there attend my coming.

[Exeunt all but RICHARD]

This scene is followed by Richard's famous soliloquy gloating over his victory. Having passed through the danger, he is exultant about his success. The emotional launch is less likely to be high enough if he knew all along this is how it would turn out. Like performances of plays, it is the energy derived from successfully playing to the on-stage crowd that now lets him turn to play directly to the actual theater audience.

On the page, because the crowd reaction is rarely noted, the powerful transformation they bring to a scene is difficult to see. On stage, however, their presence is palpable.

In this scene, the stakes are political. There are other kinds of terms, of course. When King Oberon first encounters his Queen Titania, in *A Midsummer Night's Dream*, she forswears his bed. In most productions I have ever seen, the courtiers of both unquestioningly backed up their leaders, so the fight is usually the men against the women. I have seen it performed, however, where the respective trains were obviously composed of couples, who were not happy to be parted just because their masters had a private quarrel. The scene becomes shot through with sexual frustration and takes on a fascinating new tone when played this way. Oberon and Titania are not just confronting each other, but also trying to make their case strongly and clearly enough to convince their followers that their course of action is correct. If the followers are not easily moved to the conclusion, there are many new and interesting layers of meaning in the scene. Since part of the thematic structure of the scene is accounting for disruptions in nature being caused by the King and Queen's breach, this is the perfect demonstration of it.

A Public Performance Checklist

To prepare a public scene, the following checklist may be of help:

Step 1: Prepare the scene as you would any scene, with you and your partner completing the steps outlined in previous chapters.

Step 2: When you are ready to add the crowd to the scene, begin by briefing them on their role. Define their relationship to the principals (as courtiers, bystanders, enemies, etc.). The principals should be able to declare, in a phrase or two, what is at issue and what response they want from the crowd.

Step 3: Assign any stray lines to crowd members. If their part is more than a sentence, hand them a preprepared cue script with their lines written out.

Step 4: Experiment with strategies for interacting with the crowd. The principals should try to influence the crowd. The crowd members may need an opportunity to try out some responses and see where their hearts lie. It is not important that everyone in the crowd respond uniformly, only that they respond honestly and energetically.

Figure 6. In public scenes, experiment with strategies for interaction with the crowd. In this photography of Emory University's reconstruction of The Rose Theater, note the audience members in front, beside, and behind the actors. Theater Emory's production of The White Devil, *part of their Renaissance Repertory on a reconstruction of the Rose Theater. Photo courtesy of Emory University.*

Step 5: Define winning and losing in this situation. Principals need to experiment with tactics that distract their partner from their public mission. They should see if they can keep playing to the crowd while keeping their partner from doing so.

Step 6: Experiment with big choices. Think about contemporary politics and the kinds of actions that get noticed in the public realm. Experiment to see what scale of action is required to make an impression. Notice that it is much bigger than that required to influence a partner in an intimate scene.

Step 7: Search the scene carefully for symbolic actions. Assuming or giving up crowns, kneelings and submissions, exchanging greetings, and formal challenges are some of the more common types of symbolic actions in early modern scenes. For a terrific example of this, look at the way Richard toys with turning over his crown in the deposition scene from *Richard II*. Experiment with a variety of ways of carrying out these symbolic actions.

Frequently Asked Questions for Public Scenes

Q: Forgive starting with the basics all the time, but how long should the scene be?

A: Public scenes should follow the same general guidelines as the intimate scenes did, including length and physical arrangement. At 230 lines, the example scene from *Richard III* is a good deal longer than is typical in most classroom performances. Think of it as the outer limit of scene lengths.

Q: How do we direct the crowd to respond as the scene requires?

A: Think instead of playing the scene in such a way that you and your partner contest for their loyalty. They don't need direction in a classic sense. They are learning the scene from your performance. You are directing them by playing your lines in such a way that just by doing what comes naturally, they tell the story of the scene.

Q: Should we tell them anything before the scene begins?

A: Yes. Tell them the basic situation, the relationship between the principals, and the nature of the crowd. (Are they courtiers, citizens, soldiers, etc.?)

Q: How do you rehearse the scene?

A: Just like you would any other scene, with just you and your partner working out the details. Bear in mind, however, that there will be this crowd of bystanders at a later date. Remember to allow space for them and plan them into your tactics.

Summarizing the Performance Exercises

Looking at the long arc of the performance exercises, we can see a progression. The sonnet exercises began with simple considerations of form and text, which were then lifted out of the realm of purely literary study by presenting the piece aloud to someone whose favor we sought.

Monologue exercises helped us further the initial lessons while adding considerations of situation, and, especially, character's purpose. Direct address helped us add the audience to the equation.

Intimate scenes raised us up the step to dramatic interchange, where characters seek to influence each other, while on a textual level, actors are cooperating with each other.

Public scenes helped us to see all of the previous steps in social context. The actor's circle of awareness is enlarging in each step, from self, to self and one other, to self and audience, to self and other actors, to self and others in public roles.

In the next chapter of the book, we are going to examine the nature of the theater in Shakespeare's time to better understand how these levels are built into the plays because of the conventions of his time, and then we will turn to see how these historic aspects can bring fresh excitement to the plays of Shakespeare and his contemporaries in our time.

9 Shakespeare: A Brief Biography

For a man of his time and station in life, an astonishing amount is known about Shakespeare. Compared to the facts available about most of his contemporaries (both playwrights and actors), those unearthed on Shakespeare constitute a mountain of evidence. By modern standards, however, this is still a tiny amount. Not knowing he was going to become the kind of cultural icon he has become in our time, neither Shakespeare nor his family saved any of his personal papers. Biography not yet being a literary genre, no one wrote more than a couple of sentences about him until decades after his death, by which time all the remaining oral history has to be considered suspect.

The available evidence about Shakespeare's life is almost all straight out of the public records. There is very little personal information about him, including no information of this type directly from Shakespeare himself. Except for one short excerpt from the play *Thomas Moore*, to which he was a minor contributor, and a few signatures on legal documents, there is nothing in Shakespeare's own hand. Having no diaries, no letters, and no manuscripts from Shakespeare, posterity is left with a clear outline of his life, but very little insight into the personality that lies behind it.

Early Life

Shakespeare was baptized on April 26, 1564. Tradition holds that he was born three days earlier, on April 23. That would give his life a nice symmetry since this is the date on which he died fifty-two years later. His father, John, was a prosperous merchant in Stratford-upon-Avon. When Shakespeare was four years old, his father was elected High Bailiff of Stratford, a position we would now call mayor. John was well respected and apparently prosperous, though in later years his fortunes declined markedly, possibly because of holding Catholic sympathies. Shakespeare had three brothers and a sister who survived infancy. (His youngest brother, Edmund, followed him to London and became an actor.)

The records of the local school from this period have long since vanished, but there is every reason to believe that Shakespeare attended school until about the age of fifteen. While there he would have primarily studied rhetoric and classics. His readings in Latin might well have included plays by Plautus and Seneca. It is ironic, since his work is a staple of contemporary English classes, that he would not have studied either English literature or grammar, because these subjects were not yet part of the curriculum.

Scholars have uncovered no verifiable records of his life for the years between birth and eighteen, when he was hurriedly married to Anne Hathaway, a woman eight years his senior. The rush was explained six months later by the birth of his daughter Susanna. Two years later, in 1585, Shakespeare's wife gave birth to his twin son and daughter, Hamnet and Judith.

The record sports a seven-year gap between the birth of his twins and the next entry pertaining to Shakespeare. In 1592, there is a reference to him as an upstart actor and playwright living and working in London. The seven so-called lost years between these dates have been a source of endless speculation, but without new documentary evidence, scholars are unlikely to cast any new light on them. The most logical explanation seems to be that Shakespeare continued to live in Stratford until he moved to London to pursue a theatrical career. The most favored date for this move is 1587, though this is based solely on the fact that the Queen's Men were on tour in the area of Stratford when one of their actors was killed in a duel. The possibility that they took Shakespeare on to fill the void is conceivable but conjectural. The 1592 reference makes clear that he had already earned some recognition as both an actor and a playwright, implying that he arrived in London at least a couple of years earlier.

Whenever he moved to London, he did so without his wife and children, who continued to live in Stratford. This is one of the many points about which historians wish they had even a glimpse of the underlying emotions and circumstances. Because there are no extant letters to the family, nor familial sentiments expressed in any form, there is simply no way of knowing how Shakespeare felt about living and working so far away from his family.

The London Years

After Shakespeare's first appearance in London, there are, in quick succession, many more identifiable references to him. The earliest of these are not theatrical references, however, because the theaters had been closed when the plague struck London particularly hard. Instead, the record finds Shakespeare pursuing other avenues. In 1593, he published *Venus and Adonis*, a long poem that brought him a literary reputation. A year later he repeated the feat by publishing *The Rape of Lucrece*. It was the Elizabethan equivalent of publishing two best-selling novels back to back. It is surprising, then, to find him returning to the much less respected world of the theater when the plague subsided enough for reopening of the playhouses in 1594. We tend to think, nowadays, that this was a natural course of events, but it was as odd then as it would be for a current best-selling novelist to give up the prestige associated with such accomplishment to turn to writing television scripts.

In 1594, Shakespeare became a co-owner of the Lord Chamberlain's Men, the professional group with which he would be associated for the rest of his career. Most people now think of Shakespeare primarily as a playwright, but in his own time he really earned his living as an actor. Playwrighting was not particularly lucrative, but since Shakespeare was a co-owner of the company (and an actor in his own plays, to boot), he could make it pay well if his plays were successful at the box office. He was not paid a royalty, but instead took a share of the receipts.

Shakespeare's plays *were* popular, and he made a lot of money quickly. The official records give us few glimpses into his personality, but from them, collectively, it is clear that he had a head for business. He invested his money in real estate and managed to parlay it into an immense fortune, by Elizabethan standards, when he was still in his early thirties. By 1596, he had enough money to apply for, and be granted, a coat of arms and the right to call himself "gentleman."

In midsummer of 1596, back in Stratford, the burial register tells us that Shakespeare lost his eleven-year-old son, Hamnet. Again the record is painfully silent on details. How and when Shakespeare heard, and how it affected him, are unknown.

During the next few years, Shakespeare continued to increase his fortune, his real estate holdings (including purchasing the largest house in his hometown of Stratford), and his theatrical success. He was listed as a principal actor in a play by Ben Jonson in 1598, showing that he remained an active part of the company on all fronts. Many of Shakespeare's best-known plays were written just before and just after the turn of the century. His father died in 1601, but scholars have no idea how this event affected Shakespeare.

When Queen Elizabeth, the only monarch Shakespeare had ever known, died in 1603, the future of his company was temporarily cloudy. It was a great relief that the new monarch, James I, favored the company heavily. He took it under his direct patronage, so Shakespeare became a sharer in the King's Men, as the company was then called. Technically, Shakespeare was a servant in the King's household from this time until he retired.

Shakespeare remained busy in the theater. The record shows him listed as a principal actor in a Ben Jonson play in 1603. His own plays were increasingly popular. His personal fortune climbed to the level of a modern-day millionaire, though this might have been partially due to wise investments as well.

The next several years were among his busiest as a writer and performer. The company was called to the court as many as a dozen times a year to perform before the King. Shakespeare's own plays formed a substantial part of the repertory.

In 1607, family events again loom large in the official records, though (as ever) nothing is known of their private impact. Shakespeare's daughter Susanna was married in June of that year to a prominent Stratford physician. On the last day of the year, Shakespeare's youngest brother, Edmund, an actor living in London, was buried. His funeral was more elaborate than most, leading scholars to the speculation (and it is nothing more) that Shakespeare paid for it. It is as close as we get to having any insight into Shakespeare's personal relationships.

Back in Stratford

Though he continued writing for a couple of years afterward, Shakespeare seems to have retired in about 1610, returning to Stratford. He was in his mid-forties, an enviable age at which to be able to retire, even today.

His local financial dealings continued strong, including a good deal of legal bickering over investment matters. The record continues to reflect Shakespeare's detailed interest in financial matters in London as well.

By 1615, perhaps because he sensed a decline in his health, Shakespeare began to draft his will. In early 1616 his youngest daughter, Judith, was about to be married to a man with a rather checkered past, and Shakespeare did a good deal of altering of his will at the last moment to make sure the money he was leaving her was protected from any interference by her husband.

Within a month of his last changes to the will, Shakespeare died. The cause of his death is unknown. For a man whose literary output can be so expressive, the legal documents are infuriatingly opaque. The will gives no insight into his feelings for his family or colleagues. It is written in Jacobean legalese and is thoroughly impersonal. Many have read this as a statement in itself, and perhaps it is, but it seems as likely that it is carefully devoid of personal sentiment so that it could stand unchallenged as a legal document.

From a literary point of view, by far the most significant event in the Shakespeare chronology didn't happen until well after his death. In 1623, two of his fellow owners of the King's Men, John Heminges and Henry Condell, published the complete collection of Shakespeare's plays in a volume now known as the First Folio. Nearly half of the plays in the canon had never gone into print and presumably never would have, had it not been for this project.

There is slightly more evidence available about Shakespeare's life than has been summarized here, such as a legal case in 1612 in which Shakespeare was called as a witness. It is all of the same impersonal nature, however. There are numerous stories preserved in the oral tradition and recorded in the years after Shakespeare's death, and though they give far more personal glimpses of the poet, they are all unverifiable.

Many scholars have pointed out that there is a kind of evidence available about Shakespeare's life in negative form. Because there are no records of legal troubles, imprisonment, arrests, or loans or financial borrowings (as there are in abundance for most of his contemporaries), it can be assumed that he was a generally solid and upright citizen.

Forming a Picture

In the sense modern readers desire from a modern biography, the outlines of Shakespeare's life are not anywhere near detailed enough for a full portrait to emerge. The record does not provide insight into the personality of the poet, which is necessary for a good literary biography.

A remarkable number of the records do relate to Shakespeare as a *theatrical* man, however. From just the meager facts available, a strong, clear picture emerges of Shakespeare as a theater professional. We see him as an actor, as a playwright, and even as an administrator. The publication record supports that he made a modest stab at literary fame with the narrative poems and, having achieved it, returned to the less prestigious but more financially rewarding task of making theater.

Without reading much into the record, Shakespeare's personality emerges enough to imply that he was driven for success, enough so that he was willing to make substantial personal sacrifices to achieve it. The success he desired, and which he actively protected, was as a member of a theater company rather than as an individual, however. He clearly protected the company's interests by keeping his plays out of print, so that no one else could perform them. He must not have thought of himself as a playwright seeking immortality, but as a sharer-actor-playwright who needed to make pragmatic choices if he was to earn a living.

It is often said that we don't know much about Shakespeare, but I think it more true to say that we don't know much about the relationship of Shakespeare's life to his output as a playwright. We know a good deal more about him if we think of him as a man of the theater generally.

Summary

Though everyone concedes that we have less evidence, and *much* less personal evidence, than we would like about Shakespeare's life, there is enough to form an impression of an actively committed man of the theater. The records suggest that Shakespeare didn't think of himself as a playwright writing for posterity, but as a playwright putting forth practical work for this company, which he also served as an actor and occasionally an administrator.

In the next chapter, we'll get a chance to think in greater depth about the theatrical conditions of the time and how they may have affected the plays of Shakespeare and his contemporaries.

Further Reading

For those wanting more information on this topic of this chapter, a trip to the library is apt to prove absolutely overwhelming, due to the astonishing variety of works available. The very short bibliography provided here is, rather than exhaustive, made up exclusively of recent works that I have found illuminating. More than any other list in this book, this one reflects my personal preferences, but it will give all readers a starting place.

Kay, Dennis. 1992. *Shakespeare*. New York: William Morrow.

Matus, Irvin Leigh. 1994. *Shakespeare, In Fact*. New York: Continuum.

Wilson, Ian. 1993. *Shakespeare, The Evidence*. New York: St. Martin's.

10 Shakespeare and His Contemporaries in His Time

To read and perform Shakespeare in our time requires an act of historic imagination, because the plays were written for, and originally performed in, conditions that were very different from ours. If these conditions were just the bygone artifacts of a lost era, we wouldn't care about them, but they shaped the plays in ways that give them their special enduring qualities. The theatrical attitudes and assumptions of the early modern era are still useful. To understand them is the purpose of this chapter. In the next chapter, we will look at how they apply to performing plays from this period in our own time.

Patronage

Shakespeare's choice to become an actor was not a light one. The conditions that faced him and his fellow players, like Burbage, Kemp, Condell, Heminges, and Armin, were certainly uninviting. The life of the actor was carefully restricted in Elizabethan times. The age was turbulent. Men roaming the countryside were thought to be a threat to civil peace. The social order was preserved by seeing that each man was answerable to a specific authority, who could account for his actions and his movements.

When Shakespeare was a boy, there were no permanent theaters anywhere in England. There were only a few itinerant troupes of actors, about which there was much mistrust, rather like the modern feeling against traveling carnival personnel. Most such activity was suppressed, but there was a legal loophole that made it possible for a very few professional groups to stay together. Noblemen were able to protect their servants from the laws restricting their movement, by formally entering into a patronage relationship. The nobleman was technically vouching for servants carrying out business in his name. Some nobles, as part of their suite of retainers, kept a company of actors. These actors were too expensive to maintain constantly for private entertainment, however, so they were allowed to travel about the countryside carrying documents of patronage with them when not performing in the home of their sponsor.

These troupes would swing into a town, set up a temporary theater in the town hall or an inn, and perform five or six different plays in as many days. They would then move on to the next town and repeat the pattern.

These companies of actors still had to be closely supervised whenever they arrived in a new town to perform. The duty of previewing the plays to be sure they contained no harmful material fell to each town's High Bailiff (the equivalent of our modern mayor), which was a post Shakespeare's father held when the poet was a boy. It is entirely possible that young Will was first exposed to the theater by sitting at his father's feet while the mayor carried out his censorship duties.

Later, Shakespeare himself would be subject to such scrutiny. To become an actor he had to first find a way to affiliate himself with a preexisting troupe or, at the very least, a patron. There is some speculation that Shakespeare began his professional life by joining up with a troupe as they passed through his home town. This is the best guess we have as to how he managed to solve the problem of patronage. It is a wild speculation, but we know very little about how any actor, let alone Shakespeare, first became employed during this period.

Throughout Shakespeare's life, the conditions of patronage continued to apply. For much of his career, he was a member of a troupe under the patronage of the Queen's chief of staff, The Lord Chamberlain. When Queen Elizabeth died, her successor, King James, took the troupe under his direct patronage, renaming it The King's Men. The influence of these patrons was very important to the company's survival, especially when the puritan government of the city of London sought to close them down. The patrons also supplied an important part of the company's income by paying them handsomely for command performances at court.

Patronage is tricky business. It protects the actors in some ways and obligates them in many others. It takes skill to balance the necessary flattery to one's patron with sufficient independence to create art the public might want to see and hear.

In the chapter on acting sonnets, there is an exercise designed to let you experience some of this duality for yourself. Once you have had the opportunity to feel it for yourself, you might take a few minutes to consider how it may have shaped the subject matter of the plays during this time. Many of the plays, for example, have to do with the lives of kings, and many more of the topics of leadership and the obligations of leaders to their followers.

The Profession

By the time Shakespeare was ready to join the theatrical profession as an actor, it had changed in some fundamental ways. At the same time, it continued to bear some of the more strikingly odd marks of its restricted history.

The most noticeable change of all occurred when James Burbage built The Theater, the first permanent performing house, in suburban London. This had happened only a decade or so before Shakespeare arrived in London, and it was quite an innovation. The economics of staying in one place to perform, instead of moving around from town to town, were uncertain. London was experiencing unparalleled growth, however, and the daring plan worked.

Burbage's company still performed in many ways as if it were on tour. For example, the modern pattern of putting on one play for as long as it could draw an audience was unknown. Instead, a different play was performed every day. After a few days, the cycle might be started again, but the taste for new material ran high. One company, for example, learned and performed thirty new plays in one six-month period in 1595.

In addition, the troupe did occasionally tour and frequently performed in makeshift theaters in the homes and courts of noblemen. The company's adaptability to changing performance circumstances was one great key to its survival.

The stages on which Shakespeare and his fellows performed had no scenery as such. Just as the company had done on tour, the London troupe made use of the existing architecture rather than construct anything like modern illusionistic backgrounds. Costumes, by contrast, were quite elaborate. It was not uncommon for an actor to wear a costume that cost more than his annual salary.

There were many more roles in each play than actors to fill them, so doubling and tripling of parts was common. Most actors played several parts in each play. Endurance and versatility were required of anyone who wanted to act.

Perhaps the most unusual aspect of the profession, from our modern perspective, was that women were forbidden to take part in it. All of the women's roles were performed by apprentices. Some of these young men specialized in female roles until they were in their early twenties, so it seems clear that the common presumption that they "graduated" to men's parts as soon as their voices broke cannot be right. In all probability, the imitation of women was more symbolic than realistic. Foreigners from countries where women were allowed on the stage commented that the performances were moving but not deceiving. This fluidity of gender roles was heavily explored in plays of the time, especially in Shakespeare's comedies.

To become an actor required great skills. The crowd for a play by Shakespeare, Marlowe, or Webster could number two to three thousand. They were a rowdy bunch, so the actor needed a powerful voice to be heard. The repertory demanded that actors be quick studies with good memories, too. They would be performing as many as four different roles in each of six different plays inside a single week. They might well be learning roles for a new play being introduced into the repertory the next week.

Most remarkable of all, there seems to have been almost no time for rehearsals. Actors worked closely with their fellow company members to create full performances with what could have only been very modest preparation.

We marvel at Shakespeare's abilities as an author, which are still readily apparent to us. What may not be as clear is that he was unusually gifted as a performer as well. He had to be to become a performer during such a demanding time.

The Company Structure

Shakespeare worked within a specific company structure for most of his professional life that was as unusual to his time as to ours. By 1598, James Burbage's sons, Richard and Cuthbert, had inherited their father's theatrical company and playhouse, but their lease on the land under the playhouse had run out. They were forced to disassemble the playhouse overnight and move it to another site, but, lacking capital, they took on five partners to raise the money to build a new, better playhouse partially utilizing the old materials. That playhouse was called The Globe, and one of the new owners of the company was Shakespeare. His theatrical troupe ran from that time forward as a form of business we would now call a cooperative.

Shakespeare's share of the company went up and down over the years as sharers joined and left the group, but it generally hovered at around a tenth. He was part owner, principal playwright, and supporting actor for the company from then on. Others held similar dual posts. Richard Burbage was the company's main actor but also served as administrator. Henry Condell was an actor but all of his life listed his profession as grocer, so we deduce that he may well have been concessionaire as well.

The sharers took the main roles of plays as actors and trained the apprentices that took the female roles. Whatever additional roles needed to be filled were given to freelance actors, called "hired men." The company also hired a small musical ensemble, as songs and dances were part of every play.

Companies entered into agreements with playwrights, which were mainly contracts for the authors to write to order. Shakespeare was an exception to the general rule that playwrights were not sharers in companies, but freelancers. (Shakespeare probably held his share in the company by virtue of his role as actor, not playwright.) Shakespeare was also an exception in that he did most of his writing on his own, without partners.

The chief rival company to Shakespeare's was under the control of a single manager, Philip Henslowe, who ran his business more autocratically. We have his account books for a decade, running from 1592 to 1602, which is enormously revealing about the theater of the time. He clearly hired syndicates of playwrights, sometimes as many as five at a time, to write a single play. A general scenario was established and parts farmed out. Near the end of his career, Shakespeare took part in such an arrangement, and he may have done a great deal of it under Henslowe when he was getting started, but while working at the Globe he was more his own master than was common at the time.

The Physical Playhouses and Playing Conditions

It is the playhouse structure of the time that has left the strongest marks on the plays. Starting with The Theater and continuing on through The Rose, The Globe, The Fortune, The Curtain, and all the outdoor theaters of the period are a set of common features that heavily influenced the plays.

These theaters were circular or square structures, three stories tall, with the playing area in the center, something like a modern rodeo or bullfighting ring. Around the perimeter was a seating area. There were also seats on the second and third levels. Approximately half of the center courtyard was occupied by a stage raised to the height of about five feet. This platform was supported by trestles or barrels underneath. The other half of the courtyard was standing room for audience members. The seating areas and a good deal of the stage were covered by roofs, but the standing area was open to the sky.

The wall immediately behind the stage area was reserved as a permanent backdrop. It was pierced by doors for entrances and exits onto the stage, and a central "discovery" space. About the latter, there is still a good deal of scholarly controversy as to how it operated.

The second level of the playhouse, behind the stage, was also reserved (at least at times) for playing. This is where Juliet's balcony, for example, would have been. The illustration shows many of these features, including the standing area, the raised stage, the doors on the back wall, and many other second-level playing areas.

This space was elaborately decorated architecturally but would not have changed for any performance. It was permanent. Occasionally,

Figure 7. The interior of The Globe Theater.

furniture pieces like stocks, thrones, and beds were carried onto the stage, but there was nothing comparable to a modern scene change. Nor were there intermissions. The plays took place in mid-afternoon, running for two to three hours. There was no lighting control of any kind. The plays took place in full afternoon light.

The result was a stage that was incredibly fluid. New scenes could begin as old ones were still clearing the space. Scenes in different locations might overlap each other. (Look, for example, at Romeo and his friends heading for the Capulet ball, which is being simultaneously set up on the stage in Act I of *Romeo and Juliet.*) The stage could be anywhere that the actors said it was, as there was not an illusionistic presentation but verbal suggestions of time and place.

We, in fact, usually add a piece of scenery in modern plays to suggest a location. Early modern playwrights usually added a character. Instead of bars to indicate a jail, they would have brought on a man carrying keys to play the jailer. Same effect, different method.

It was possible to get on and off a stage like this very quickly. Because there are multiple entrances, large crowds can sweep on rapidly, and just as quickly, disperse.

The main condition of the physical theater was that the audience was extremely close, and very involved. They were not sitting quietly in the dark, as in modern theaters, but were milling about freely in the same illumination as the actors. Actors didn't treat this as a distraction, but actively involved the audience. They spoke directly to them in moments of soliloquy. They frequently performed presentationally to them. They interacted with them to a degree we would find remarkable in our time.

Throughout the period, there were some performances in indoor spaces as well. These were generally smaller spaces catering to a more elite crowd. Performances were held in the evenings in candlelit venues. These spaces were more like modern theaters than the great public spaces outdoors, but many of the same plays were performed in both, so the playing conditions were not vastly different. Shakespeare's company owned a space called the Blackfriars, which may have been the theater he had in his mind when writing his late plays. The chief difference seems to have been more elaborate machinery, which allowed for more miraculous effects, like gods appearing and banquets disappearing. (Look, for example, at *The Tempest* and *Cymbeline* to see such effects in the plays.) Overall, however, it is the public playhouses outdoors that shaped the acting and writing styles of the times.

The Nature of the Theater

The net result of all these conditions was that Shakespeare's theater was a place that deeply engaged the audience and actively sought their imaginative cooperation. Look again at the Chorus speech that begins *Henry V*, as presented in Part II, for the plea it makes to the audience.

With no scenery or lighting, the theater was much less a visually realistic place and much more a verbally influenced, imaginative one. It was possible, on this stage, to create a night scene by suggesting the darkness and adding torches or candles, though, in fact, the play was being performed in the late afternoon in full sunlight. It was equally possible to suggest hiding places and set pieces (like the "wall" to the Capulet orchard that Romeo "leaps") through the use of language alone.

In subject matter and geography, the stage extended far beyond the ordinary realm of realism. (Shakespeare, for example, wrote only one play, *Merry Wives of Windsor*, that could be said to involve the everyday life of ordinary citizens of his time.) Instead, the audience's flights of fancy were employed to carry them to far away times and places and, in some cases (like the magical forest of *Midsummer Night's Dream*), to places that can't really be said to exist.

Gender was verbally constructed, like so much else in the theater. Young men and boys played girls, often in disguise as boys. To the audience, they were what they said they were.

There is a great deal of unresolveable debate about the acting styles of the time. It is widely held that they were based in rhetorical and declamatory practice, but the passionate intensity called for in the plays seems to call for a strong emotional technique as well. We can never really recover the style, but I am among those who think it might have far more modern validity than is generally believed by many scholars.

The plays clearly reflect the theatrical conditions of the time. They are often sweepingly epic, calling for large numbers of characters in many locations, times, and planes of existence. Faustus[1] can call forth the devil. Oberon can be invisible to mortals. Tamburlaine can conquer half the world in two hours. Antony can lose as much as quickly. This is possible because the stage is a relatively neutral space, which can be verbally reset at a moment's notice. One man can stand, as Chorus asks in *Henry V*, for a million. Or one man could stand for one woman. It was a brilliant time because it was so ripe with possibilities. If a playwright could imagine it, then actors could perform it.

Of course, our theatrical conditions are not like this any more. In the next chapter, we'll think a little about the plays of Shakespeare and his contemporaries in *our* time. We are apt to do very different performances from those of their time, but there are still ways in which we might honor the basic conventions of the period because they still can serve us well.

---

exercises

Pacing Off a Globe Footprint

The Globe, the theater with which Shakespeare was most closely associated, was a twenty-sided polygon, with a 100 foot exterior diameter and a 75 foot interior. The stage would have extended about half-way out into this central circle. Using a ball of string, a 20-foot tape measure, and a set of wooden stakes, go to a large outdoor space and lay out a "Globe." Consult the picture on page 136 to help you visualize the space.

Though this may seem like a tall order, the original builders did, in fact, lay out the foundation plan with no more tools than these. They had only their measuring rod, their skill at geometry, and their knowledge of building skills to guide them. See if you can figure out how they did it. Stake out the interior circle and a stage. Imagine 1200 people (the actual capacity of the first floor) inside the circle you have laid out.

Finding a Globe

Look around at buildings in your area that have multistoried atria and find the one that most closely matches the Globe. You are looking for a three-story atrium built around a central space of about eighty feet. It is highly unlikely that you'll find an exact match, especially since square spaces are much more common than "round" ones in our time, but you can probably find a good approximation. Go stand in the "courtyard" and imagine this as a staging place. If you are part of a class or a study group, send members to the various levels of balconies and call a few lines to them. Experience the various dynamics of performing in such a space.

Note

1. In Marlowe's *Dr. Faustus*. The rest of the paragraph refers to Oberon from *A Midsummer Night's Dream*, Tamburlaine from Marlowe's *Tamburlaine the Great, Parts I & II*, and Antony from *Antony and Cleopatra*.

11　Shakespeare and His Contemporaries in Our Time

Shakespeare is not only the most successful playwright who ever lived, he is still, today, the playwright who is most produced on the stages of the world. In any given year, the thirty-eight plays that make up his canon are seen by more live theatergoers than the works of any other person. Recent films of his plays extend that audience even further. When you add in the millions of readers, you reach incredible numbers.

None of Shakespeare's contemporaries can rival these numbers, but (often because of an interest in the period associated with Shakespeare) many of their plays are still produced on a regular basis, four hundred years after their creation.

Early modern literary works, then, are still very much a part of the repertoire. Though it is often said that an actor can't make a living doing classics, the truth is that it is pretty hard to make a living *not* doing them!

It is not just that these plays are such a prominent part of the repertoire that should draw us to them. For actors, they are so rewarding to perform! Because of their scope, their relish of language, their brilliantly imaginative approaches, and their challenging intellectual content, they remain the pinnacle of opportunities.

It is not an accident that this literature has lasted so long and remained so popular. It has many qualities that have helped it to remain both current and powerful. This chapter will discuss several of these. It will attempt to outline some of the major acting concerns and how actors can continue to address them. It will begin by addressing the single most important and, ironically, complicating of these—the plays' great openness to interpretation.

The pragmatic necessity of Shakespeare's time, to keep the staging of plays neutral and invest the production energy in imaginative approaches, has resulted in plays that are infinitely malleable. Shakespeare's plays (and, of course, the plays of his contemporaries) have lasted in part because they were open enough to changing circumstances to be able to continue to hold the stage in the decades, and then centuries, after they were originally written. They still have this capacity. In our time, the hallmark of Shakespearean production is the variety of approaches to the plays. It cannot be said that there is a Shakespearean "style" in the way that one might say there is an approach to David Mamet, or Andrew Lloyd Weber, or Wendy Wasserstein. Shakespeare plays can sometimes look like musicals, sometimes like gritty realistic dramas, sometimes like multicultural improvisations. Productions can be feminist, or Marxist, or romantic. They can be controversial or conservative. They are sometimes immense displays of spectacle, sometimes stripped down to a half dozen actors and a chair.

There is no single approach that works, but there are guidelines within which we can work. The following suggestions are just that: ideas about what to hold in mind while preparing to act the plays. None of them should be considered an airtight rule. Instead, it is more useful to think of them as avenues of exploration. Ultimately, a performance is a joint product of the actor and the conceptualizer of the production (usually, but not always, the director). This chapter is about what you might bring to the table, with the final selection a matter of negotiation.

Qualities of the Period

If one were to be transported through some mystical (or technological) device to Shakespeare's lifetime, there are attitudes toward life and toward performance that would help you succeed. It would undoubtedly help you to aspire to a range of skills that we might now find contradictory: accomplishment as both a poet and a warrior and as both a scholar and a lover. It would also help you to be highly fashionable, to the point of social aggressiveness. Your chances of social recognition would increase with your ability to live life to its extremes. Intense passions were the order of the day. Musicality was valued. Scientific curiosity was new but esteemed.

It was a heady time. The excitement of the "new world," with all its potential for discovery and profit, was just breaking into the public consciousness. The changing social order opened opportunities for classes of men (like Shakespeare) who formerly would have been held firmly in place.

In a few words, the celebration of life was larger. Especially in the artistic realm, where newly optimistic humanism reflected the scientific advances and economic gains of the time, the representation of life was more vigorous. In current performance, even when the play is moved out of period, these larger-than-(contemporary)-life qualities are still useful. The size and pace of life is written in such a way that it is a quality of the characters, not just of their time.

While preparing a performance, approach things first with an Elizabethan- or Jacobean-scaled attitude. You can always tone down if the particular production circumstances demand that of you, but it is hard to scale up if you have no experience with the larger realm.

Indulgence of the Language

Using and relishing language looms large in early modern drama. Starting with Marlowe's "mighty line," an incredibly vigorous iambic structure with a relentless pulse, the plays of the period are highly invested in strong, active use of words. This is not just a matter of lining them up in verse forms or using a large word where a short one would do. It is an almost uncontrolled impulse to explore and celebrate the power of the rapidly expanding English vocabulary.

There is a certain vocal skill that can help most performances, of course, but what is suggested here is more attitudinal than technical. It is a matter of falling in love with speaking. As an actor, even in very modernist performances, the desire to explore the words and their power is advantageous.

A Strong Voice

There is the technical side of the previous point, which is so frequently employed that I feel it only fair to list it separately. Most productions of early modern plays still depend on actors with above-average vocal skills, as both speakers and singers. Vocal power is not enough in itself, but in combination with other acting skills, it is often a deciding factor in casting. Cultivate your voice, and care for it.

Subsidiary Skills

There were a number of guides to being a successful member of court that were written in Shakespeare's time, the best-known of which is Castiglione's *The Courtier*. This guide, and those like it, enumerated a range of skills that one needed to advance in the social circles of the time. These guides were the early modern equivalent of the pervasive self-help and personal-improvement books aimed at the business executive (and would-be executive) of our time.

Not surprisingly, many of the same skills touted in courtiers' guides were written into the plays, where actors could model them for the general public while playing courtiers. The ability to dance well, fence well, sing well, play an instrument well, and write at least passable verse was admired. All of these show up in the plays. Ophelia is able to say of Hamlet, for example, that he is:

> The courtier's, soldier's, scholar's eye, tongue, sword,
> Th'expectancy and rose of the fair state,
> The glass of fashion and the mould of form,
> Th'observed of all observers . . .

The more of these areas you have spent time on, the more you have to offer to a production.

An Openness to the Complexities of Gender

Because of the original production circumstances, in which a gender fluidity was a given quality of the performance, many of Shakespeare's characters (and some of his contemporaries', though

Figure 8. Because of the original production circumstances, a gender fluidity was a given quality of performance, as in this meeting between Viola and her twin brother Sebastian in Twelfth Night. *Photo by Joan Marcus, courtesy of The Shakespeare Theatre, Washington, DC.*

not as frequently) have a gender complexity about them. They may conceive of themselves in ways less rigidly codified than sex roles sometimes dictate in our time. Gender-bent performances (where men play women and vice versa) can be intensely illuminating and theatrically interesting far beyond their novelty value.

For young students, this can be an intensely psychologically threatening area, because it is hard to separate gender roles from sexuality, but the latter is not the point here. There are good reasons to avoid what Professor Evelyn Tribble has dubbed the "tall, white guy theory of casting,"[1] in which the most traditional figure in any group is given the role of authority. Of course, we live in a time that is questioning such role assignments, so there is a social reason for this exploration, but there is also a literary one. Gender ambiguity is written into the plays, and it is one of the imaginative qualities

Figure 9. Theater Emory's historic reconstruction performance of The White Devil, *part of their Renaissance Repertory on a reconstruction of The Rose Theatre. Photo courtesy of Emory University.*

that still has the most power to compel attention and thought in the modern theater.

Some Common Production Approaches

There are, of course, as many individual approaches to producing Shakespeare as there are productions, but there are some trends that frequently recur with which it is useful to be acquainted. The following approaches are neither definitive nor exhaustive, but may give you some ideas about the more common ones currently employed in the modern theater.

Historic Reconstruction
This approach is listed first, though it is employed less frequently than you might guess. In historic reconstruction, the original playing conditions are recreated. This might mean historically accurate costuming and reconstructions of Elizabethan playing spaces, but it doesn't always. This line of thought dates to William Poel's productions at the turn of the twentieth century and is getting some attention at the newly reconstructed Globe on the bankside in London.

Other groups that are interested in historic conditions, like the Shenandoah Shakespeare Express (a touring Shakespeare company based in Virginia), are often influenced by the underlying conventions more than the surface conditions of historic performance. The Shenandoah company, for example, performs in conditions in which the actors are very close to the audience, and they choose to interact with them. They eschew scenery, limiting themselves to what props they can carry on and off. They perform with the audience in full light, even when they perform in theaters with modern lighting capabilities. In this sense, they are faithfully recreating some of the most important historic conventions, but they also perform in tennis shoes, T-shirts, and jeans. They are recreating what they believe to be the dynamic of early modern performance, not the appearance.

Plays Reset to New Time Periods, Including the Present
The most typical approach to Shakespeare in our time is to reset the plays in recognizable but anachronistic time periods. Kenneth Branagh's film treatment of *Hamlet*, which, by the appearance of the costumes at least, is set in the Edwardian period, might serve as an example. These time periods include almost all the periods subsequent to Shakespeare's, up to and including the present. *Hamlet* might again serve as an example, this time using the Court Theater's 1989 production starring Aidan Quinn, which was set in the same year as the production. Its most famous moment was when Hamlet spray-painted a graffiti "to be or not to be" on a wall of the set to begin his soliloquy. Productions using this device often employ the conventions of theatrical realism for most of their production choices.

Plays Employing a Visual Eclecticism
Another common approach is to visually mix many time periods and performance styles in a single production. The photograph of The Shakespeare Theatre's production of *Troilus and Cressida* illustrates this. In it, the characters are wearing clothing that suggests ancient silhouettes, but they have many modern pieces about them. Hector (in the foreground) is wearing a mesh shirt, for example. The warriors in the background are wearing gas masks, though they are fighting the Trojan War.

Productions like this are often visually spectacular but generally nonrealistic. Their mixture of visual elements must be considered

Figure 10. A common approach is to visually mix many time periods and styles in a single production, as here in Troilus and Cressida. *Photo by Joan Marcus, courtesy of The Shakespeare Theatre, Washington, DC.*

symbolically or abstractly, and these same conventions are often employed in the acting styles. A juxtaposition of contemporary casualness and classical artfulness creates a jarring, jazzy style.

A Timeless, Empty Space

Since Peter Brooks' groundbreaking production of *A Midsummer Night's Dream* in 1969, one of the most prominent approaches to Shakespeare is to set it in a modern version of the early modern neutral platform.

Sometimes called the "white box" approach, this production strategy focuses attention on the actors by reducing the set to a periodless minimum. These productions are usually vocally oriented, featuring polished verse speaking. Sometimes character is subordinated to fine voices, and although the production values may be high, the designs tend to be simple and direct.

Issues-Oriented Productions

The last major approach is the most complex. It is governed by a conceptual concern with foregrounding a specific issue or idea. Recently, the best of these productions often feature feminist and/or multicultural concerns and interpretations. The world-famous productions by Ariane Mnouchkine with France's *Théâtre de Soleil* and, in the United States, the Shakespearean productions of JoAnne Akalaitis serve as examples.

Casting of these productions is often gender-bent (whereby actors are cast without reference to gender, or actors are cast in roles traditionally played by members of the opposite gender to make a point) or colorblind (whereby actors are either cast without reference to racial characteristics, or race is used to make a point). The acting styles employed in such productions can vary widely but generally tend heavily toward the nonrealistic.

---

some performance explorations

---

1. Imagine yourself, like the Connecticut Yankee in King Arthur's Court, to be transported in time, in this case from your time to Shakespeare's. Imagine that you instantly acquire the confidence and size of the period. Read a speech with your newfound attitude. Seek to succeed by the standards of the time. See how it is different from your usual self.

2. Invent a new word to describe a specific new concept. Don't just generalize or make a funny sound combination, but attempt to do what Shakespeare did with great regularity: add a word to the language. You may have to create it by using parts of words you already know or sounds that suggest its meaning. Share your word

with a few other people. Speak it out loud. Use it in a sentence. See if you can make clear what it means, without resorting to defining it, or worse, miming it!

3. With a partner of the opposite gender, read a Shakespeare scene. Read it again, switching roles. See what you can learn about gender constructions with this simple exercise.

Note

1. In a personal communication. Dr. Tribble is a superb teacher of Shakespeare and an adventurous explorer of casting possibilities. I have learned a great deal from watching her perform many nontraditional roles, especially of figures in the histories.

12. About Editions

Among the most surprising aspects of performing early modern plays is discovering that there are no "definitive" editions. This is true for all plays by Shakespeare and most of those by his contemporaries. The various editions available differ highly from each other. You cannot be sure that the words on the page of your copy of, say, *King Lear* or *The White Devil*, will be the same as the ones in a different edition that a scene partner might bring to a rehearsal. Often, the differences are a few words here and there, but sometimes the variations are so large that you seem to be looking at different plays. Whole speeches, even scenes, may vary.

Though it may, at first, seem odd, many of our most basic assumptions about what the text of a play is may not apply to early modern plays. Scholar Stephen Orgel has demonstrated that plays in this period weren't the kind of direct expression of the author that we now assume. He points out that plays were commissioned by theater companies, which often dictated the subject matter, sometimes split up the acts and scenes for composition by different authors, cut and pruned the text for performance, and authorized rewrites and revisions (sometimes even years after the initial performance). Authors had little say in the matter. They didn't own the plays on which they worked. Likewise, when the plays were sold to a printer, the author had no rights; the concept of copyright did not yet exist. The printer might revise the play in numerous ways for publication without consulting the author or authors.

Furthermore, since the play went into print only *after* it had found some success on the stage, the idea of a script as a guide to performance was completely unknown. The printed play was, instead, a record of performance. In most cases, that record was not of the author's opinion or desires, but rather of the enterprise as it had been collectively carried out.

Plays were, in short, collaborative ventures in which many people had a hand. Shakespeare might, at first, seem an exception, since he was a co-owner of the theater company for which he wrote, but as Orgel has brilliantly argued, even Shakespeare was subject to the same conditions. He was just in on more parts of the collaboration.

Because there are no extant examples of Shakespeare's notes, rough drafts, or finished, handwritten copies, it is now completely impossible to get back to his "original text," if such a thing ever existed. The very few examples of handwritten "texts" available from his contemporaries also do little to solve the problem. Editions of plays were, and are, subject to the involvement of many people. None is perfect.

For actors, the question of the dependability of the text is not idle scholarship or arcane speculation. It is a vital matter of what words and actions, even what interpretations, will hold the stage.

The simple rule of thumb is that everything is a "version," and you will need to be involved in the selection of the best and most appropriate choice for your performances. To do so intelligently, you need to understand a little bit about the nature of the various versions that are available.

Early Modern Printings

The closest things to "official versions" are the various Renaissance versions of texts published in the lifetimes (or soon thereafter) of Shakespeare and his contemporaries. These editions reflect the certain involvement of many collaborators in some degree, and may involve substantial intervention by the printers. Because spelling and punctuation rules had not yet stabilized at the time these editions were printed, they often contain a considerable subjective element. Sadly, many were also printed badly and contain a large number of typographical and compositional errors. Nonetheless, these versions contain much of interest to the contemporary actor.

Quartos

During this period, a play was most often published in a form known as a *quarto*. Quartos were paper-bound books just about the same size as modern acting editions of plays, just a bit larger than the typical contemporary paperback novel. Usually, a quarto contained only a single play. The cost of such a book was roughly equal to the ten, or so, modern dollars that a current edition might cost and was therefore available to the ordinary reader. (Editors often abbreviate references to quartos with the letter "Q" followed by a number, such as Q1 or Q3. As will be explained later, there were sometimes several quarto editions of a play printed in the period. The number refers to the edition being referenced, in chronological order of publication.)

Generally speaking, theater companies sought to prevent their plays from being published, because once a play was in print, anyone could perform it. The company held a monopoly on "performance rights" only through keeping plays out of circulation.

Quarto editions of plays often show signs of the lack of cooperation from the theater companies. Some of these editions contain heavily garbled versions of texts that are now familiar. As much as a third of the material of the play is sometimes omitted, and what is there is often in a very different order than it appears in other editions. Scholars now assume that quartos in this condition reflect the possibility that the text was reconstructed from memory by actors from plays in which they had appeared, were taken down in shorthand during a performance, or were otherwise acquired through dubious means. Quartos that have these characteristics are known as "bad" or "short" quartos.

Other quarto editions seem much more reliable. These "good" quartos were apparently printed from the author's handwritten rough drafts of the plays, called the "foul papers," or from their final drafts, called "fair copies," or in a few cases, from promptbooks. What induced an author or theater company to cooperate in this publication is a matter of speculation, but in Shakespeare's case, it seems that "good" quartos of some of his titles frequently appeared not long after "short" editions. Perhaps he or his company felt obligated to preserve his literary reputation by allowing the publication of accurate versions to refute the earlier (stolen?) editions.

Folios

Shakespeare's friend and rival, Ben Jonson, pioneered the publication of authors' collected works in folios. Folios are much larger than quartos, with a page size about the same as a contemporary newspaper folded in half. Folios were much more elaborate and expensive publications, which were usually bound in nice leather covers soon after purchase. Because of their expense, they were not used for individual plays, but only for substantial collections.

Shakespeare's collected works were published under the guidance of two of his fellow actors seven years after his death. About half of the plays that now form the Shakespeare canon appear for the first time in what has become known as the First Folio. (This is abbreviated, according to the system explained earlier, as F1.)

Of course, modern commentators are enormously thankful for this edition, or these plays would be lost to us forever. Of equal interest are those plays that had previously appeared in one or more quarto editions. The Folio often differs not only from "bad" quartos, but also from "good" quartos in a great many ways. *Hamlet* and *Romeo and Juliet*, for example, contain hundreds of lines that appear in one or the other but not both editions. The differences between the quarto and Folio versions of *King Lear* are so great and irreconcilable that many modern collections consider them separate plays and print both!

Which edition to follow is often a matter of judgment and taste rather than any absolute dictum. There are often multiple "good" versions of plays dating from the author's lifetime, offering several different and equally viable alternatives. Sorting through alternatives can be very complicated. After a brief discussion of facsimile versions, we will turn to the subject of modern editions that help sort through the many possibilities.

Facsimiles

Almost any academic library will have some early editions available in *facsimile* (something like photocopy) editions. Shakespeare is, of course, more commonly available than his contemporaries, but facsimile versions of works by his contemporaries exist. Even some of Shakespeare's quartos can be a bit hard to come by, but Shakespeare First Folios are widely available.

Renaissance texts are more than a little difficult for beginners to deal with, but these editions contain much that is of interest to actors. Despite the old spellings, unusual typographical conventions, and inconsistent speech headings, there are reasons to persevere. At the simplest level, it is nice to be able to see the raw materials underlying modern editions. On a higher plane, early modern punctuation and capitalization is much more rhetorically based than our current grammatical models. They are, therefore, often far more suggestive of effective delivery patterns than are modern editions, which are no longer punctuated with the speaker in mind. There is no evidence to support the current fad for ascribing all the punctuation, capitalization, and spelling choices in the Folio directly to Shakespeare (and much evidence to contradict it), but these aspects of the Renaissance editions can be extremely stimulating because they are closer to a performance model, even if they are the work of scribes, compositors, and printers, rather than Shakespeare himself.

Most actors who regularly perform in early modern plays own a facsimile copy of Shakespeare's Folio and regularly consult it for these suggestions of delivery patterns and other matters. For plays by other authors, facsimile versions of the plays in libraries are often consulted.

Modern Editions

Most productions of early modern plays are built around modern editions of texts, albeit often in conjunction with consultation of Renaissance editions. Contemporary editors are often experts with years of experience in reading early modern literature and thinking about its conventions. They can be invaluable when sorting through variant texts. The typical practice of a modern editor is to establish the Renaissance version that they find the most sound (for reasons that ought to be clearly delineated in their notes) and then compare all other versions to it. They will modernize spelling, punctuation, and act or scene divisions and then, on a literally word-by-word basis, decide on the best choices available (in their opinion).

Modern typographical conventions, contemporary spelling, and regularization of line, scene, and act numbering offer great convenience. The real value of modern editions lies in the contemporary scholarship and sometimes extremely helpful explanatory notes and supporting essays. With a few cautions, you too will probably find modern editions helpful and convenient.

First, whether or not the edition says so, someone edited the text. When you buy an edition, the main thing you are paying for (since Shakespeare is not getting a royalty) is the experience and judgment of the editor. Mostly, you get what you pay for. Be wary of inexpensive editions that list no editor or contain no contextual materials that explain the principles that guided the editor. Often, these are reprints of variations edited as long as a century ago, when editors felt free to intervene in the text extensively and subjectively. Lines they didn't understand, phrases they found offensive, even unusual scansion patterns were changed to suit the editor's whim.

Modern editors are apt to be much more careful about editing, based on consistent principles. Spelling may be modernized, but not randomly. Careful attention is paid to punctuation, spelling, stage directions, speech headings, and other matters that may have great bearing on the final performance. These are usually regularized according to modern grammatically based rules. These are changes, but changes that often result in making the text more accessible, especially to young actors.

This is not to say that any modern (and expensive) version is good and any old one is bad. It *is* to say that you need to examine editions carefully. Look for a statement of editorial principles. These are rarely deathless prose, but they tell you what you need to know: specifically, what the editor was trying to accomplish.

Among contemporary editors, many seek to shape a text that makes for good reading for scholars and students who will study the play on the page. Fewer seek to shape the text with attention to performance issues, but those are the best editions for actors. The 1986 *Oxford Shakespeare* (which serves as the basis for the 1997 *Norton Shakespeare*) is an example of a text in which the editors have paid great attention to the theatrical viability of what they are doing.

Their editorial principles specifically recognize the collaborative nature of early modern texts and validate the contribution of actors. Not surprisingly, therefore, it is an edition that is widely trusted by actors. Because of the quality of the notes, Arden editions are also often found in the rehearsal room.

Modern editions typically supply a good deal of supporting material that explains the sources of the text, the main lines of contemporary scholarly thought on the play, the history of the work as a text and in performance, and brief biographical material about the author. All of this can be useful to the actor. A typical edition of a single play costs around ten dollars. This is a reasonable investment for the information you get in return. The play is usually printed in a handy paperback size that can easily be carried in rehearsal. Shakespeare's plays are most often printed in single-play editions. Other early modern authors more often appear in volumes that contain two or three plays together. Many actors also own an edition of the complete works of Shakespeare, such as the Riverside or the Bevington, which they bring to rehearsals for the purposes of consultation, even if it is too heavy to carry around on stage.

Finally, there is an increasing availability of so-called electronic versions on the Internet for the cost of printing them out. These, like more conventional versions, come in a variety of edited forms, some much better than others. The biggest advantage an electronic version holds is the ability to print it out at large type sizes. The tiny (cost-saving) type sizes of published editions can hamper a rehearsal.

There is no definitive answer as to which version to use, but there are certainly some versions that are much better than others. Most actors find a comfortable modern edition from an editor or series they know and trust and then cross-reference it with an early modern facsimile version. Just be sure that any actors you are working with have a chance to consult with you so that you are working from the same basic versions. Discuss any variations that you plan to introduce into your performance so that they thoroughly know the lines and cues of the scene.